THE CASE FOR LONG-TERM VALUE INVESTING

THE CASE FOR LONG-TERM VALUE INVESTING

A guide to the data and strategies that drive stock market success

JIM CULLEN

HARRIMAN HOUSE LTD
3 Viceroy Court
Bedford Road
Petersfield
Hampshire
GU32 3LJ
GREAT BRITAIN
Tel: +44 (0)1730 233870

Email: enquiries@harriman-house.com
Website: harriman.house

First published in 2022.
Copyright © Jim Cullen

The right of Jim Cullen to be identified as the Author has been asserted in accordance with the Copyright, Design and Patents Act 1988.

Hardback ISBN: 978-0-85719-947-8
eBook ISBN: 978-0-85719-948-5

British Library Cataloguing in Publication Data
A CIP catalogue record for this book can be obtained from the British Library.

THE CASE FOR LONG-TERM VALUE INVESTING

The purpose of this book is to help investors deal with the challenge of successfully investing in the stock market by using a value discipline.

The book has 38 short chapters. While a book could be written on the subject of each chapter, the objective here is to present a series of concise introductions to the topics, to give investors a feel for the markets.

CONTENTS

BACKGROUND

I STARTED INVESTING IN the stock market when I was an officer in the Navy, aboard the aircraft carrier USS *Essex*. It was 1961 to 1964 and during those four years the market moved steadily higher, which led me to conclude that picking stocks was easy and maybe even fun.

When I got out of the Navy in 1965, Wall Street was booming. Then, as now, wild speculation dominated and value investing was totally out of favor. A whole new generation had taken interest in the stock market, as the memories of the Crash of 1929 and the Depression of the 1930s faded into distant history.

As enthusiasm for stocks intensified, the large brokerage firms opened branch offices all over the country. This is when I started working at Merrill Lynch in their new Wall Street office. Most of us there were in our energetic mid-20s. "Millennials" was not then a term, but we were the equivalent.

Every day our offices were mobbed with individual investors trading stocks and commodities. They yelled and cheered as prices crossed the office ticker tape.

All of a sudden in 1968, as the Dow was about to break through 1,000 for the first time, the market lost its momentum, and the next five years produced two major recessions that resulted in two stock market collapses. By the end of 1975, when the dust finally settled, the Main Street brokerage offices had been shut down and many of the brokerage firms and their brokers went down with them. Wall Street, the center of the financial world just a few years before, was a ghost town. So much for easy and fun.

It was during this time that two events occurred. First, Ben Graham gave a speech in 1974 pointing out that he had a simple new way of analyzing stocks. This method focused on investing for the long term and applying a discipline of price/earnings, price/book and dividend yield. We can summarise this Graham approach as long-term value investing.

Second was a study by Paul Miller, published in Barron's, which showed how the cheapest stocks on a P/E basis dramatically outperformed the highest P/E stocks and the market as a whole. Again, Miller's study demonstrated the efficacy of value investing.

These two events wound up being the basis ten years later for the foundation of my firm, Schafer Cullen, which now manages approximately $20 billion dollars using the long-term value strategy.

JIM CULLEN
New York, 2022

ABOUT THE BOOK

THIS BOOK IS intended for the average investor, who has historically been at a big disadvantage in dealing with the stock market. And it is easy to see why. It's because of the almost irresistible temptation and herd instinct to buy stocks when they are very popular and at highs, and sell them when they are out of favor and at their lows. The purpose of this book is to help the investor overcome that temptation.

The book is divided into seven sections. The **first section** covers market history over the last 100 years. The purpose is to show how volatile and unpredictable markets are over time.

The **second section** is the core of the book, which is the investment strategy itself. Here we focus on Ben Graham's advice to be a long-term investor and apply the value disciplines of price/earnings, price/book and dividend yield.

Section Three, Market Timing, is extraordinarily important because trying to time the market has often been referred to as the silent killer of long-term performance.

In **Section Four** we look at the stock selection process—here we depart from the theoretical and deal with the tricky venture of picking stocks.

Section Five outlines how the discipline strategy can be applied to various investing styles.

Section Six is about understanding the market, following Graham's comments that the reason why most investors don't do well in the market is because they tend to overreact and do not really understand the workings of the market.

In the last section, **Getting Started**, we provide some advice for new investors. I believe that for those readers who are new investors, this could be the most important chapter in the book.

SECTION ONE

THE BATTLE

We begin with The Battle.
A history of 100 years in the stock market.

My reason for starting with this history in
Section One, ahead of the investment strategy
to be found in Section Two, is to help investors
appreciate how consistently volatile and
unpredictable markets are over time.

1

A Brief Market History—
The Last 100 Years

The 1920s

THIS DECADE WAS dubbed the "Roaring 20s" as the stock market boomed, speculation ran wild, and the NYSE was more a casino than an exchange. Large investment pools dominated the market and manipulated stock prices for short-term gains.

Where Are the Customer's Yachts? was a best-selling book at the time. The idea for the book came out of a conversation at a Wall Street club where some members looked out at all the stockbrokers' yachts in the harbor. At some point one of them asked innocently: "Where are the customers' yachts?" This pretty much summed up the decade.

The poster child of the market was RCA, the world's largest manufacturer of radios. Early in the decade, virtually no one owned a radio; but soon enough millions of radios were going to be sold in the US and around the world. Because of RCA's phenomenal growth prospects, the stock price soared from $5 to $120. As predicted, sales were strong, but the stock price got way ahead of the company's earnings.

When the market crashed in 1929, RCA collapsed to $5 a share—while the average stock on the stock exchange dropped 80%. Most investors, large and small, got wiped out. Legend has it people on Wall Street were jumping out their windows.

Radio Corporation of America Stock Price
(January 1925–December 1935)

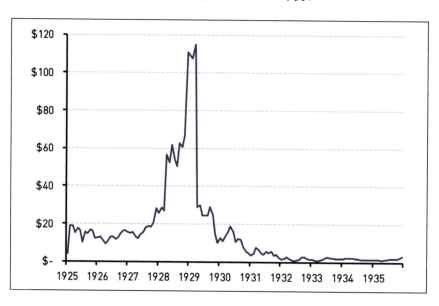

Source: The Wall Street Journal.

The 1930s

The 1930s, the decade of the Great Depression, featured little or even negative economic growth as unemployment reached a stunning 25%.

To address the jobs crisis, the government injected massive amounts of fiscal stimulus into the economy and created programs like the Civil Conservation Corps. But a second leg down in the stock market in 1935 killed any hope of a mid-decade recovery.

Meanwhile, the stock market was still considered a place only for speculators, not investors. By the end of the decade, the Wall Streeters' yachts were also gone.

The 1940s and 1950s

During these two decades, there was still little interest in the stock market and trading was very light. The public was out of the market. In the mid-1940s, corporate earnings started to improve because of the stimulus provided by defense spending during World War II.

Due to the continuing lack of interest in stocks, valuations had become attractive, as P/E multiples of most stocks dropped to historic lows. The overall market was selling at 10x earnings, and the dividend yield was 5%. The attractive valuations had investors gradually coming back into stocks.

The 1960s

By the early 1960s, confidence finally started to return to the market, as the traumatic experience of the 1930s began to fade into distant memory.

By the late 1960s, public enthusiasm for stocks again reached fever pitch. Major firms like Merrill Lynch and EF Hutton set up retail brokerage offices on Main Streets all over the country.

New investors then, as now, were completely oblivious to risk, as leveraged hedge funds and high-profile mutual funds were rapidly formed to respond to the demand for new issues and small cap stocks that were all the speculative rage. A legendary Wall Street character some called "Two-A-Day" Charlie Plohn issued at least two dubious small cap underwritings every day. The public clamored for more and, in almost every case, these small companies wound up worthless.

The most popular trading stocks of the time were *conglomerates*. These were highly leveraged vultures disguised as companies, specializing in hostile takeovers and acquisitions. They were the darlings of the market and every day were the most actively traded stocks on the exchange.

Some of the popular names were Leasco Data Processing, Gulf & Western, Solitron Devices, LTV, Litton Industries, University Computing, and National Student Marketing—each with its own wild story.

For retail investors, margin accounts became the new way to play the market in general and buy the hot stocks in particular. Going on margin allowed investors to borrow money against their portfolios in order to buy more stock. As long as the market was going up, adding leverage to your account dramatically increased performance. And so margin accounts became almost irresistible to the average investor.

It was during this wild time that I began my career at Merrill Lynch in their new office on Wall Street. The place was so mobbed with retail investors every day we had to put up a Plexiglass wall to separate the boisterous crowd from the brokers. Because of all the interest, we set up rows of permanent seats, a Dow Jones ticker, a research library, ashtrays, and even a spittoon.

Our brokerage office, like most at that time, looked like a British betting parlor. There was a party happening and everybody was having fun. For good reason the period was dubbed the "Go-Go Era" by Adam Smith, who wrote a best seller, *The Money Game,* about all the goings-on.

For extra excitement, the Dow was approaching 1,000 for the first time. The press was aggressively trumpeting this anticipated event. The following photo shows our Merrill Lynch office (with me in the back).

Dow 1,000 by Year-End Seen Possible, **The New York Times,**
October 20, 1968

Cornell Capa © International Center of Photography / Magnum.

Given the wild enthusiasm over stocks, it is hard to believe the market not only didn't break through 1,000 then, but would not do so for another *14 years*.

The 1970s

Following the Go-Go years, the 1969–1970 recession wiped out the conglomerates, and margin accounts, while also clearing out the crowds from the brokerage offices. History might say stocks were flat during the 1965–1982 period. But if you were part of it, the market was anything but flat—which can be seen in the following chart.

Dow Jones Industrial Average (1964–1982)—Anything But Flat!

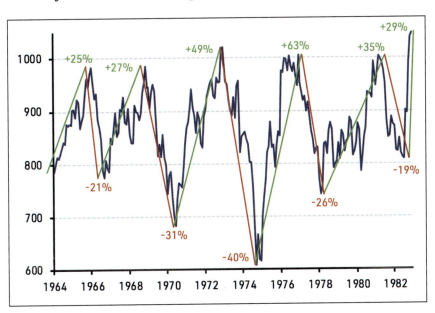

Source: Bloomberg; SCCM Research.

The major New York banks had not participated in the wild speculation of the 1960s. Until the early 1970s, the big banks and financial institutions stayed away from the market because of their disastrous experience brought on by the Crash of 1929 and the Depression of the 1930s.

However, among institutional investors there was a developing belief that this was a new era for stocks because of the unlimited growth prospects for a group of high-quality companies. Among them were IBM, McDonald's, Xerox, Polaroid, Eastman Kodak, Proctor & Gamble, and Avon Products. These and 43 others became known as the *Nifty Fifty*.

At this point the big financial institutions, eventually followed by the public, began aggressively buying these Nifty Fifty companies. The assumption was that their growth prospects were so phenomenal that one could buy at any price because their growth would eventually justify it.

The assumption proved to be wrong. Valuations reached levels that turned out to be unsustainable. In January of 1973 the market rolled over and dropped 50% the next year. We then witnessed the worst recession since the 1930s and the Nifty Fifty bubble became history.

The cover from a December 1974 issue of *The Economist* magazine showed a hot air balloon composed of flags of France, Japan, Germany, the US and the UK crashing onto a rocky landscape—illustrating just how hopeless the future for the market had become. Interestingly, December 1974 represented the bottom of the market.

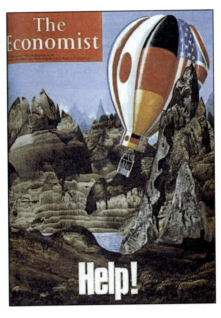

© The Economist Newspaper Limited, London December 21st, 1974.

To illustrate how devastating this recession was, following is an underwriting release for American Motors—a well-known auto company at the time. It might seem inconceivable that 100% of the underwriters, some of them over 100 years old, would be wiped out through bankruptcy or merged out of existence in a few short years.

This advertisement is not an offer to sell or a solicitation of an offer to buy these securities.
The offering is made only by the Prospectus.

1,000,000 Shares

American Motors Corporation

Common Stock
(Par Value $1.65⅔ Per Share)

Price: $12.75 per share

Copies of the Prospectus may be obtained in any State only from such of the
undersigned and others as may lawfully offer these securities in such State.

Kuhn Loeb & Co.   White Weld & Co.

Blyth & Co. Inc.   Eastman Dillon, Union Securities & Co.   Glore Forgan & Co.

Halsey, Stuart & Co. Inc.   Harriman, Ripley & Co.   Hornblower & Weeks-Hemphill, Noyes

Loeb, Rhoades & Co.   Stone & Webster Securities Corporation

A.G. Becker & Co.   Clark, Dodge & Co.   Francis I. DuPont & Co.   Hallgarten & Co.   Hayden, Stone

W.E. Hutton & Co.   Lee Higginson Corporation   F.S. Moseley & Co.   R.W. Pressprich & Co.

Reynolds & Co.   Shields & Co.   Spencer Trask & Co.   G.H. Walker & Co.   Walston & Co.

Auchincloss, Parker & Redpath   F. Eberstadt & Co.   Estabrook & Co.   Faulkner, Dawkins & Sullivan

Goodbody & Co.   Laird   McDonnell & Co.   Mitchell, Hutchins & Co.   New York Hanseatic Corporation

New York Securities Co.   F.S. Smithers & Co.   C.E. Unterberg, Towbin Co.   Van Alstyne, Noel & Co.

June 16, 1969

Source: American Motors Corporation, *June 16, 1969.*

The 1980s

As the decade began, stocks were still down and the inflation rate climbed to 13.5%, the highest in the post-war period. Fed chairman Paul Volker stepped in and took interest rates to 20%. The move killed both inflation and the market, producing the double dip recessions of 1981 and 1982.

The recession was not only unexpected; it was also the most serious since the Great Depression and had a severe effect on financial institutions. Banks had been active in real estate lending and speculation just as the economy soured. The rate of bank failures was the highest since the 1930s. Continental Illinois, the nation's seventh largest bank at the time, failed and had to be bailed out. The reason for the rescue was fear that its collapse would also topple some of the biggest banks in the country like Bank of America, Manufacturers Hanover Trust and even Citibank.

As fear reigned on Wall Street in 1981, the *Bank Credit Analyst*, considered the most influential institutional research publication, issued a throw-in-the-towel opinion piece.

The publication stated: **individuals and companies were falling behind on their interest payments, and bonds, stocks, real estate and commodities were all being liquidated and the trend was not likely to end soon.**

They went on to say: **the disaster in the banking area plus the burden on states and municipalities indicated a long recession and that for the weakest sectors of the economy, the worst was yet to come.**

This doomsday scenario was dated October 1981, which turned out to be one of the greatest times to buy stocks in market history.

The aftermath of the two recessions set the stage for a recovery, as stock prices became extremely oversold. Many of the Nifty Fifty stocks were down 80% from their 1973 highs and overall valuations were at one of the cheapest levels in market history. Meanwhile, corporate earnings were improving, which helped the Dow to finally break through the 1,000 level in 1982.

During the recovery, investors eventually started to appreciate the attractive valuations. Renewed enthusiasm was building for stocks. Because they had been getting out of the market for 10 years, there weren't many new sellers around and exposure to stocks was at one of the lowest levels ever. Even so, a gradual build-up of speculation was developing.

By the mid-1980s, the stock market was constantly making new highs and investor enthusiasm was once again revving up. It was during all the renewed excitement that we first began to hear the term "melt-up market." That is a market that goes up for more than 200 days in a row with no more than a 10% correction. You'll find a whole chapter on melt-up markets later in the book.

Despite the public's enthusiasm for stocks, institutional investors were still nervous, as they remembered the 1970s collapse of their Nifty Fifty stocks. So they wanted to make sure they had some downside protection. To achieve it, Wall Street quantitative analysts came up with a supposedly foolproof way of using derivatives to give investors a hedge that would guarantee all the downside protection they wanted. It was called *portfolio insurance*.

But it turned out the hedges were not foolproof. In 1987, there was a correction triggering the portfolio insurance, starting a run on the market that produced a 25% one-day drop. This one-day sell-off remains the worst in market history. Investors were stunned. *Barron's* front cover of October 26, 1987 highlighted the event.

Unlike today, floor brokers at the time were responsible for the liquidity and price stability of stocks. They became the heroes when they got together with management of the Dow Jones 30 companies and convinced them to aggressively buy their companies' stock the next day on the open.

Even though institutions and the public continued to sell the following day, the Dow Jones index finished up for the session and all the news headlines were about how the Dow had recovered and not about how almost all the other stocks were down. The news headlines about the gain in the Dow stabilized the market, which gradually started working its way higher. By the end of the year, new highs were being made.

The 1990s

During the early 1980s when stocks were out of favor, real estate became popular as an investment alternative. This marked the beginning of the use of the term "alternative" as a substitute for equities.

By the end of the 1980s, enthusiasm for real estate was getting overdone. An example of the speculation was the Florida condominium market. Large condominium complexes were referred to as "see-throughs" because nobody lived there and the condos were all owned by speculators.

The frenzy in the real estate market saw the 1990s begin with a banking and real estate crisis. As illustrated in the chart below, the number of US bank failures in this period exceeded the failures of the 1930s recession.

History of US Bank Failures

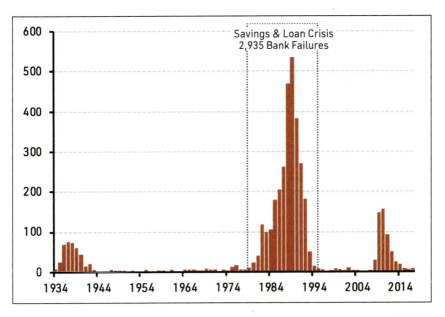

Source: Federal Deposit Insurance Corporation (FDIC).
Includes bank failures and assistance transactions.

The biggest losers were the small banks, mainly the mom-and-pop savings and loan (S&L) operations. These were set up by local businesspeople, primarily to finance real estate deals, and were part of life in almost every town in the country. The S&L industry pretty much got wiped out by the crisis, as did many of the small banks. There was no bailout for mom and pop, but the government did set up a vehicle called the Resolution Trust Company, which took in, marked down, repackaged and resold much of the underwater real estate that was forced into liquidation.

By 1995, the financial industry was recovering from the real estate and banking problems. At the same time, there were breakthroughs in technology that started to attract notice. Investor enthusiasm for the new tech companies eventually became so extreme that it led to a belief in a "new paradigm." The most popular stocks—Intel, Microsoft, and Apple, among them—led to the creation of a new index called NASDAQ.

Gradually, as we neared the end of the decade, stock prices started reaching valuation levels only seen a few other times in history. Stocks climbed higher and higher, not because of fundamentals, but because security analysts constantly raised price targets for the stocks, and that alone pushed prices higher. The public was back into the stock market. *BusinessWeek* acknowledged the boom right at the market highs with a front cover stating "The Boom."

The strength of the tech stocks affected the popular S&P 500 index because high-fliers were gradually being added to the index, producing one of the index's highest valuation levels in history.

By the end of the 1990s, the NASDAQ was selling at 65x earnings and the S&P 500 at 28x earnings.

The 2000s

In 2000 the market rolled over and in the years that followed the wildly popular NASDAQ dropped 80%, even though tech company earnings increased during the same time span. This fall of the NASDAQ is illustrated in the following chart. The result was much like the aftermath of the 1920s and of the Nifty Fifty era, where the problem was not with the companies themselves but rather with their valuations.

The performance of the S&P 500, heavily weighted with the popular tech stocks, was also affected—its performance was dramatically worse than the more reasonably priced value stocks for many years. From 2000–2005, the S&P 500 was down −2.3% on an annualized basis and −11.0% cumulatively, while value stocks (measured by bottom 20% by P/E) was up +17.4% annualized and +122.8% cumulatively.

NASDAQ Composite (1998–2004)

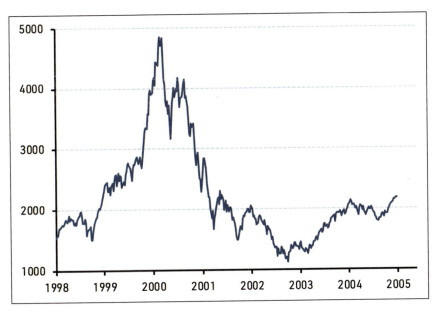

Source: Bloomberg.

If the tech sell-off in 2000 wasn't bad enough, the terrorist attacks of September 11, 2001 delivered one of the biggest shocks in US history. The market collapsed and the stock exchange, which was directly impacted by the destruction of the World Trade Center, had to be shut down.

History shows that when the market is already down and a major event like 9/11/2001 occurs, more often than not the stage is set for a market low, which is what happened when the market bottomed initially in December of 2001. The market then rallied for almost a year, rolled over again, and made a final low in September of 2002. A *BusinessWeek* cover entitled "The Angry Market," showing a roaring bear, was published two months prior to this.

The market rallied 100% from those September 2002 lows over the next few years. However, the good feeling didn't last long because by 2007 we were confronted with another banking crisis. This resulted in the stock market having its biggest drop since the 1930s.

During the boom year of 1995, a gang of Wall Street insiders had convinced the Clinton administration that the economy would be a lot stronger if it got rid of some of the financial restrictions on Wall Street. One restraint was the Glass-Steagall Act, which was adopted in the 1930s and had been responsible for a certain amount of market stability for 50 years. The removal of Glass-Steagall, which separated lending and trading operations, along with the repeal of the uptick rule, which limited short selling, set the stage for massive trading operations by the banking firms and the use of exotic derivatives, all which led to the market collapse of 2008/2009.

The sell-off was legendary and there was fear that the unintended consequences could be so bad as to cause the entire financial system to collapse. As a result, the big banks and auto companies had to be bailed out by the government. The following *Fortune* cover, albeit from a later date, conveys the mood at the time.

The 2010s

This decade was a beneficiary of the extremely negative decade of the 2000s and the bounce back from the 2007/2008 sell-off with the help of government stimulus. As in other recoveries following extended bear markets in 1930 and 1974, investors were slow to come back into equities. The demographic group of young adults, the millennials, showed no interest at all in buying stocks.

The tone of the Clinton/Trump campaign in 2016 also left the public feeling negative about the stock market. Even so, because the market remained oversold, it kept gradually working its way higher, as many of those worried about the election, who had gone to cash, started to drift back into the market. The millennials still showed no interest.

Suddenly in January 2018 the stock market exploded, producing one of the strongest Januarys in market history. This was driven by the millennials coming into the market, lured by the excitement over the cannabis industry and the Bitcoin craze. Retail firms like Schwab and Fidelity were suddenly swamped by new investors and despite reservations about the election of Donald Trump the market went on to make new highs.

2020

As the new decade began, millennials' excitement over Bitcoin and cannabis stocks had expanded to market speculation, encouraged by commission-free trading from firms like Robinhood, resulting in a casino-like environment.

Meanwhile, enthusiasm for FANG stocks (Facebook, Amazon, Netflix and Google) continued to build, as it did for other tech companies including Tesla and Apple. These stocks became the centerpiece for the development of a new technology boom and were becoming the new NASDAQ. The concentration became so extreme that at midyear 2020, the 10 largest tech stocks were up $900 billion while the other 2,600 or so stocks in the NASDAQ were actually down $300 billion.

In late 2019, Covid-19 emerged and spread all over the world in 2020. How Covid-19 plays out will have an impact on the market in the U.S. and worldwide. Fortunately, as we will see throughout the rest of the book, investing with a discipline and being a long-term investor has helped investors absorb the various challenges.

And this is where we are up to at the time of writing. It remains to be seen what comes next. However, if this survey of the last 100 years teaches us anything, it is that investing is a challenge.

SECTION TWO

THE VALUE
STRATEGY

This section lays out the foundation of the long-term value investing approach by examining the three investment disciplines price-to-earnings, price-to-book, and dividend yield.

We also discuss the importance of dividends and earnings in the process, a comparison of value vs. growth and why value outperforms, and finally the importance of sticking with the approach for the long term.

2

The Value
Disciplines

Price/Earnings—Price/Book—
Dividend Yield

I N EARLY 1975, Wall Street was recovering from the 1973–1974 recession—the worst since the 1930s. Stocks were down 50% from their highs. Investors were in a state of shock and had no interest in the stock market.

Ironically, it was in early 1975 that Benjamin Graham, known as the "Father of Value Investing," gave his final interview, one that summed up his 60 years in the investment business. Because few at the time showed any interest in the market, the Graham interview got virtually no attention, but what he said was new and forms the cornerstone of the investment strategy outlined in this book.

The essence of what Graham said was that he had worked out a value strategy he believed would consistently outperform all others, and, applying the strategy, you could forget everything else.

The key, he said, is to invest with a value discipline—price-to-earnings, price-to-book, dividend yield—and to invest for the long term. The approach has consistently worked, with the only exception being occasional bubble-like periods, which we discuss later in this section in Chapters 5 and 6.

Let's look at the two elements of the strategy.

The Strategy

1. Invest with a Discipline

Over the years the Achilles heel of the investor has been overpaying for future growth, i.e., buying stocks when they are popular and expensive. As Graham advised, to avoid making that mistake, you must apply a price discipline. The disciplines he recommended were price-to-earnings, price-to-book, and dividend yield. Investors should screen stocks using one or more of these three ratios, in order to buy cheap companies and avoid overpaying.

When looking for value stocks, we use the three criteria as follows:

1. *Price-to-earnings*: We look for companies in the bottom 20% of the index when ranked by price-to-earnings.

2. *Price-to-book*: We look for companies in the bottom 20% of the index when ranked by price-to-book.

3. *Dividend yield*: We look for companies in the top 20% of the
   index when ranked by dividend yield.

2. Invest for the Long Term

The second part of Graham's strategy is as important as the first.
Graham said it is crucially important for investors to understand
that markets are completely unpredictable over one-, two-, three-,
or even four-year periods. However, if the discipline is applied for a
longer term, performance will be driven more by fundamentals and
earnings rather than other factors like momentum, fear, and greed.
Although Graham didn't specify a time span, using a five-year period
tends to smooth performance. We can see this in studies of market
data—as shown below.

A Look at Market History

Let's look at some data on Graham's three recommended disciplines
dating back to 1968. We can compare how each of the disciplines
performed relative to the S&P 500.

We can look at the performance for the cheapest 20% of stocks
by price-to-earnings, the cheapest 20% by price-to-book, and the
highest 20% on a yield basis—all rebalanced annually. The results
are that all three disciplines give investors a big edge over time.

The following table summarizes the data. Three observations
can be made:

1. The market (as represented by the S&P 500) is wildly erratic on a
   year-to-year basis.

2. The three value disciplines outperform overall (see averages at table bottom).

3. Value outperforms in the majority of individual years, except in bubble periods.

The Three Disciplines (1968–2020)

Years	S&P 500 Index (%)	Bottom 20% by P/E (%)	Bottom 20% by P/BK (%)	Top 20% by Yield (%)
1968	11.0	30.5	37.3	27.3
1969	−8.4	−16.5	−23.7	−16.6
1970	3.9	12.8	2.9	12.1
1971	14.3	10.5	18.9	10.7
1972	18.9	8.0	6.8	10.3
1973	−14.7	−14.8	−14.2	−13.9
1974	−26.5	−10.9	−5.9	−20.0
1975	37.2	59.3	62.4	64.3
1976	23.9	48.0	56.2	42.1
1977	−7.2	8.5	4.5	4.0
1978	6.6	14.1	7.1	3.1
1979	18.6	30.8	32.3	20.1
1980	32.4	32.8	19.2	17.4
1981	−4.9	17.5	14.9	17.7
1982	21.5	27.9	39.4	31.0
1983	22.6	28.1	43.0	33.4
1984	6.3	17.1	5.1	12.6
1985	31.7	34.2	20.3	32.4
1986	18.7	32.1	10.1	18.4
1987	5.3	−6.2	9.9	−1.4
1988	12.5	28.0	30.9	20.5
1989	31.7	22.7	21.3	26.2
1990	−3.1	−15.2	−24.4	−17.5
1991	30.5	47.9	54.4	43.3
1992	7.6	16.7	32.4	18.3

Years	S&P 500 Index (%)	Bottom 20% by P/E (%)	Bottom 20% by P/BK (%)	Top 20% by Yield (%)
1993	10.1	16.9	22.7	16.0
1994	1.3	2.3	−0.2	−2.3
1995	37.6	41.6	37.4	36.3
1996	23.0	18.9	16.4	16.3
1997	33.4	37.0	30.7	27.9
1998	28.6	−0.3	11.5	8.7
1999	21.0	7.0	10.8	−2.3
2000	−9.1	24.2	22.2	15.4
2001	−11.9	16.2	14.6	11.1
2002	−22.1	−8.9	−17.7	−8.4
2003	28.7	38.6	57.0	36.8
2004	10.9	22.3	23.8	15.3
2005	4.9	15.9	11.6	3.8
2006	15.8	18.1	20.9	23.2
2007	5.5	−0.7	−12.5	−1.4
2008	−37.0	−39.1	−47.3	−39.9
2009	26.5	52.8	65.1	45.0
2010	15.1	20.5	23.0	20.7
2011	2.1	1.3	−6.9	12.8
2012	16.0	16.0	24.0	12.6
2013	32.4	42.7	45.2	30.2
2014	13.7	11.8	8.8	19.8
2015	1.4	1.4	−0.2	−0.5
2016	12.0	17.8	24.9	19.6
2017	21.8	17.9	13.7	9.8
2018	−4.4	−13.6	−16.6	−5.6
2019	31.5	26.3	22.9	24.1
2020	18.3	−4.0	−9.4	−6.1
Average Annualized Total 1968–2020	10.3	14.6	13.9	12.4

* See appendix for calculation methodology.

Five-Year Perspective

While the results overall are convincing, you can see that on a year-to-year basis, performance is very unpredictable. However, using a five-year time period goes a long way to eliminate the volatility. As you can see in the table that follows, when we look at the performance of the cheapest 20% of stocks by P/E, there was only one negative five-year period in 50 years. This was 1969–1973.

Performance of low P/E stocks in five-year periods (1968–2020)

Period	S&P 500 Bottom 20% by P/E	Period	S&P 500 Bottom 20% by P/E
1968–1972	8.00%	1993–1997	22.50%
1969–1973	−0.90%	1994–1998	18.70%
1970–1974	0.40%	1995–1999	19.70%
1971–1975	7.60%	1996–2000	16.60%
1972–1976	14.10%	1997–2001	16.10%
1973–1977	14.20%	1998–2002	7.00%
1974–1978	21.10%	1999–2003	14.30%
1975–1979	30.70%	2000–2004	17.40%
1976–1980	26.10%	2001–2005	15.80%
1977–1981	20.40%	2002–2006	16.20%
1978–1982	24.40%	2003–2007	18.20%
1979–1983	27.30%	2004–2008	0.20%
1980–1984	24.50%	2005–2009	4.80%
1981–1985	24.80%	2006–2010	5.60%
1982–1986	27.70%	2007–2011	2.40%
1983–1987	20.10%	2008–2012	5.60%
1984–1988	20.00%	2009–2013	25.30%
1985–1989	21.20%	2010–2014	17.70%
1986–1990	10.50%	2011–2015	13.70%
1987–1991	13.10%	2012–2016	17.20%
1988–1992	18.10%	2013–2017	17.60%
1989–1993	16.00%	2014–2018	6.40%
1990–1994	11.90%	2015–2019	9.00%
1991–1995	23.90%	2016–2020	7.80%
1992–1996	18.60%		

We have observed that whenever a difficult five-year period occurs, the following five-year period turns out extremely strong. This is because stock market history shows that earnings tend to double approximately every ten years, so when performance is flat for any five-year period, stocks tend to make up for this in the next five-year span. This relationship between earnings and stock prices is explored further in Chapter 3.

This pattern of a strong five-year period following a poor five-year period can be seen in the following table. For example, looking at the three most difficult periods: 1969–1973 was –0.9% and the following five-year period was +21.1%; 1970–1974 was +0.4% and the following five-year period was +30.7%; and 2004–2008 was +0.2% and the following five-year period was +25.3%.

Performance Following Difficult Five-Year Periods

Poor Five-Year Periods	Bottom 20% by P/E	Following Five-Year Periods	Bottom 20% by P/E
1968–1972	8.0%	1973–1977	14.2%
1969–1973	–0.9%	1974–1978	21.1%
1970–1974	0.4%	1975–1979	30.7%
1971–1975	7.6%	1976–1980	26.1%
1998–2002	7.0%	2003–2007	18.2%
2004–2008	0.2%	2009–2013	25.3%
2005–2009	4.8%	2010–2014	17.7%
2006–2010	5.6%	2011–2015	13.7%
2007–2011	2.4%	2012–2016	17.2%
2008–2012	5.6%	2013–2017	17.6%

Other Studies

The record is clear: the strategy of investing with a discipline and for the long term gives investors an edge over time. Many other similar studies over the years highlight the same results.

An early statistical study based on P/E multiples was done by Paul Miller of Miller Anderson. When he did the study, Miller was the head of research for Drexel Burnham. The results, seen below, were published in *Barron's*. What they show is the lowest P/E decile stocks outperformed the highest in every time period—one year, two years, three years, and nine years. They even outperformed the median P/E stocks (deciles 5 and 6).

Miller Study: P/E: More is Less? The Ups & Downs of Average Annualized Total Returns (1967–1976)

	Stocks Grouped by Multiples	Quarter (%)	One-Year Period (%)	Two-Year Period (%)	Three-Year Period (%)	Nine-Year Period (%)
Highest P/E Decile	1	−1.6	1.1	0.0	1.1	1.4
	2	2.0	3.4	2.6	−0.7	3.2
	3	2.3	3.0	1.8	−0.5	5.4
	4	2.8	2.8	1.9	−2.4	5.9
	5	4.8	5.4	5.6	2.2	5.8
	6	5.1	7.1	6.7	2.3	4.5
	7	9.4	7.5	7.4	3.0	6.9
	8	11.8	8.4	8.7	4.1	8.4
	9	11.8	9.6	11.4	5.1	7.0
Lowest P/E Decile	10	19.4	10.2	11.4	8.9	8.9

Source: Drexel Burnham/Barron's, 1977.

Earlier Studies

A question I often get is: did the low P/E discipline always work, i.e., in earlier market times?

There are many other studies dating back over different time periods. Below is one of these by Francis Nicholson, published in the *Financial Analysts Journal*. His study focused on the 100 largest blue-chip industrials and covered the period from 1937–1963. Once again, the lowest P/E quintile outperformed in every single time period. Nicholson's study, combined with Miller's, and with the results from our studies shown earlier in the chapter, illustrate the outperformance of value for the 83 years from 1937 to the present.

Francis Nicholson's Five Uneasy Quintiles (1937–1963)

	Stocks Grouped by Multiples	1 Year (%)	2 Years (%)	3 Years (%)	4 Years (%)	5 Years (%)	6 Years (%)	7 Years (%)
Highest P/E Decile	1	3	11	21	31	46	65	84
	2	6	14	24	35	50	65	83
	3	7	18	30	43	60	77	96
	4	9	22	34	48	65	82	100
Lowest P/E Decile	5	16	34	55	76	98	125	149

Source: Financial Analysts Journal, *February 1968.*

Summary

There are other studies we could cite over various time periods using different indexes. They all show that investing with a value discipline over the long term gives investors a decided edge. This represents the core of the investment philosophy described in this book.

3

Earnings:
Why Stocks Go Up

THE MAIN REASON stocks go up over time is because stock prices follow earnings, which go up over time.

Earnings tend to double, irregularly but on average, about every ten years. This happens because corporate managers make adjustments to address challenges they encounter, like recessions, inflation, pandemics, international crises, and much else, to keep earnings on the rise. And we investors are the beneficiaries.

The following chart, beginning in 1940, shows how corporate earnings, as represented by operating earnings per share (EPS), in the aggregate have grown steadily despite 13 recessions in this period (indicated by the light blue bars in the chart).

S&P Operating EPS and Index Price (1940–2020)

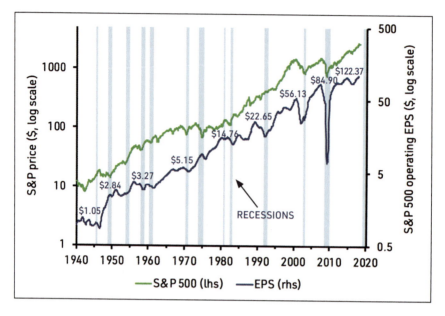

Source: SCCM, 2021.

Earnings Doubling

The following table illustrates how S&P earnings tend to double about every ten years.

S&P 500 Earnings (1932–2018)

Year	EPS	Years to Double	Year	EPS	Years to Double
1932	$0.41		1984	$16.64	11
1936	$1.02	4	1995	$33.96	11
1948	$2.29	12	2006	$81.51	11
1963	$4.02	15	2018	$150.00	12
1973	$8.16	10			

Source: Standard & Poor's, 2019.

Earnings Yield

Another explanation of the connection between earnings and stock prices can be found by looking at earnings yield. "P/E" is a ratio and tends to be a Wall Street term, while "earnings yield" is more of a layman's term and enables investors to compare the actual returns from stocks with other investment types, like real estate or bonds.

Earnings yield represents the return on your investment. For example, a stock selling for $10/share and earning $1/share has an earnings yield of 10% (the stock has a P/E of 10x). If those earnings double to $2/share, the earnings yield rises to a 20% return on the original investment.

This example helps one realize the importance of earnings relative to a stock's price, rather than what is going on in the stock market.

4

Dividends

After looking at how well earnings did over the last 60 years, let's now look at dividends over that same time period.

The following chart shows dividend growth compared to the S&P 500. We can see that dividends were smoother and less volatile than earnings growth from 1940 to 2019. It is also clear that over the last 12 recessions, dividends actually went up in virtually every period. The only exception was the 2009–2010 recession when banks were forced by the government's TARP program to cut or eliminate their dividends. As you can see, since then, S&P 500 dividends are back to all-time highs.

S&P 500 Dividends/Share (1940–2020)

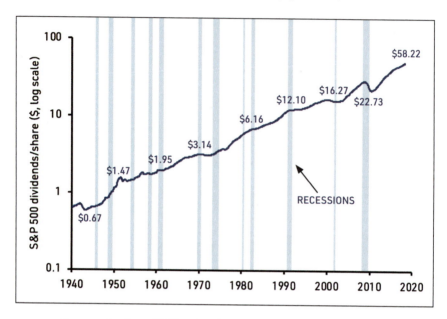

Source: Robert Shiller, Ned Davis Research, Standard & Poor's,
and Morgan Stanley Research, December 2020.

Below we take a closer look at two of the major down periods.

The first is the 1973–1975 recession. It lasted almost two years and stock prices dropped approximately 50%. In addition, corporate earnings also went down about 50%. As we discussed in Chapter 1, "Market History," Wall Street during this period was in a state of total chaos. Margin accounts were being liquidated every day and many of the major Wall Street firms were going out of business. In this environment it is hard to believe that S&P 500 dividends, represented by the green line, moved up over this entire period.

S&P 500 and Dividends/Share (1972–1976)

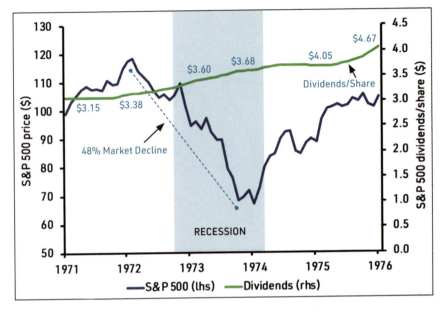

Source: *Bloomberg, 2021.*

A second example was the "Double Dip Recession" of the early 1980s. This period lasted for almost three years and was when Fed Chairman Paul Volker pushed interest rates up to 20%. Financial markets got hammered and stocks sold down to one of the lowest P/E multiple levels in market history. Meanwhile, once again, dividends for the S&P 500, the green line, went up throughout the entire period.

S&P 500 Index and Dividends/Share (1979–1982)

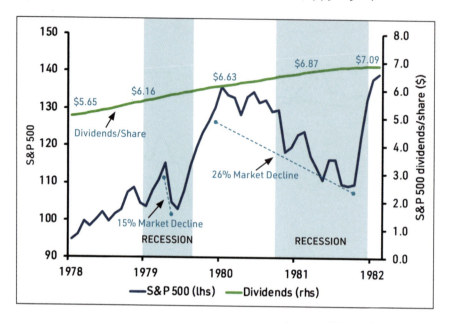

Source: Bloomberg, 2021.

5

Value vs. Growth

THERE HAS ALWAYS been a debate about value investing vs. growth investing.

What makes the debate lopsided is that growth gets all the favorable media attention while value often enough runs up against stories in the financial press about the "death of value." Have you ever seen a headline announcing "the death of growth investing"?

Given this, the results of the study below might surprise you.

The study measured performance based on rolling five-year returns. As we have seen, the use of that time span smooths out the volatility of year-to-year performance. With that time span in place, we can compare value (bottom 20% on a P/E basis) against growth (top 20% on a P/E basis) dating back to 1968.

Value consistently and dramatically outperformed growth, except for the Tech Bubble and recent FANG/social media boom of 2014–2020.

And even in these two anomalous periods, the outperformance by growth was minimal.

Meanwhile, when value outperformed, it consistently tended to be by a much larger margin. As you can see in the following table, over the entire span of 50 years, value outperformed by a substantial 50% (15.43% versus 9.43%).

S&P 500 Lowest vs. Highest P/E Stocks (1968–2020)

Rolling 5-Year Periods	Top 20% by P/E (Growth)	Bottom 20% by P/E (Value)	Value Outperforms	Growth Outperforms
1968–1972	3.25%	7.96%	4.71%	
1969–1973	−3.80%	−0.88%	2.93%	
1970–1974	−6.13%	0.42%	6.55%	
1971–1975	3.05%	7.59%	4.55%	
1972–1976	4.35%	14.06%	9.71%	
1973–1977	−0.75%	14.18%	14.93%	
1974–1978	5.59%	21.06%	15.48%	
1975–1979	18.97%	30.73%	11.77%	
1976–1980	17.20%	26.06%	8.85%	
1977–1981	10.15%	20.38%	10.22%	
1978–1982	20.34%	24.39%	4.06%	
1979–1983	27.09%	27.31%	---flat*---	
1980–1984	16.42%	24.53%	8.10%	
1981–1985	13.96%	24.79%	10.83%	
1982–1986	15.18%	27.74%	12.56%	
1983–1987	10.50%	20.06%	9.56%	
1984–1988	6.30%	20.04%	13.74%	
1985–1989	14.06%	21.16%	7.10%	
1986–1990	4.23%	10.52%	6.29%	
1987–1991	10.95%	13.05%	2.10%	
1988–1992	12.25%	18.11%	5.86%	
1989–1993	13.12%	15.98%	2.85%	
1990–1994	9.63%	11.85%	2.22%	
1991–1995	20.74%	23.95%	3.21%	

	Rolling 5-Year Periods	Top 20% by P/E (Growth)	Bottom 20% by P/E (Value)	Value Outperforms	Growth Outperforms
	1992–1996	17.43%	18.65%	1.22%	
	1993–1997	16.98%	22.50%	5.52%	
	1994–1998	17.78%	18.66%	---flat*---	
Tech Bubble Melt Up	1995–1999	24.19%	19.72%		4.47%
	1996–2000	17.73%	16.63%		1.11%
	1997–2001	10.47%	16.09%	5.62%	
	1998–2002	−1.68%	7.01%	8.68%	
	1999–2003	4.81%	14.30%	9.49%	
	2000–2004	1.82%	17.38%	15.56%	
	2001–2005	3.97%	15.77%	11.80%	
	2002–2006	9.79%	16.16%	6.36%	
	2003–2007	18.97%	18.16%	---flat*---	
	2004–2008	−7.44%	0.23%	7.67%	
	2005–2009	−0.05%	4.81%	4.86%	
	2006–2010	3.16%	5.61%	2.45%	
	2007–2011	−0.59%	2.41%	2.99%	
	2008–2012	3.13%	5.64%	2.51%	
	2009–2013	27.24%	25.27%		1.97%
	2010–2014	17.46%	17.68%	---flat*---	
	2011–2015	13.80%	13.70%	---flat*---	
Social Media Melt Up	2012–2016	17.75%	17.19%	---flat*---	
	2013–2017	15.99%	17.57%	1.58%	
	2014–2018	7.74%	6.36%		1.38%
	2015–2019	9.92%	8.98%	---flat*---	
	2016–2020	11.82%	7.79%		4.03%
		Annualized Returns		Average Outperformance	
	51 years 1968–2020	9.70%	14.60%	7.15%	2.59%

* flat = less than 1% difference.
Source: Standard & Poor's, SCCM Research.

So Why Doesn't Everyone
Use a Value Strategy?

Back in 2005 after we originally conducted the study to compare the track records of value and growth, we wondered why everybody doesn't use the value approach, since the outperformance of value is so commanding and persistent.

To answer the question, we did a second study to track the performance over the 20 years prior to 2005. The results are shown in the following table. You can see that while value had the best performance during the whole period, it was the best in only two of the 20 years. In other words, for 18 years, some strategy other than value was doing better and getting all the media attention.

In Chapter 34, "The Wall Street Quilt," we will look at a further update of this study.

Ranked by Performance (1985–2004)	Annual Performance	Number of Years	
		Best	Worst
1 Large Cap Value	14.50%	2	0
2 Foreign Stocks	11.80%	6	7
3 Small Cap Stocks	11.30%	6	6
4 Large Cap Growth	11.10%	4	1
5 Bond	8.80%	2	6

Large Cap Value: Bottom 20% of stocks in the S&P 500 by P/E.
Foreign Stocks: Morgan Stanley EAFE.
Small Cap: Russell 2000 Small Cap Index.
Large Cap Growth: Top 20% of stocks in the S&P 500 by P/E.
Bonds: Lehman Brothers Aggregate Bond Index.

6

Why Value
Outperforms

L OOKING AT THE last chapter, "Value vs. Growth," it's hard to believe that value not only consistently outperforms growth, but usually does so by a large margin. As we mentioned, you would never know it because all the excitement and publicity about growth stocks when they are in favor drowns out the steady success of value.

The reason for value's dramatic outperformance is because when the growth stocks finally roll over, their downside tends to be long and steep. Meanwhile, value tends to only modestly trail growth in the up periods, but meaningfully outperforms when growth goes out of favor. The key to the growth vs. value study is analyzing performance on a rolling five-year basis, which as we have shown, smooths performance and sheds light on the growth/value debate.

In the following chart we highlight when growth stocks have had their most dramatic periods of popularity. This is when the index gradually becomes increasingly overweighted with a few high-multiple growth stocks. The Nifty Fifty period and the Tech Bubble were periods when the most popular stocks became a huge part of the S&P 500 index: 23.1% of total market capitalization in the former period and 18.0% in the latter.

On the far right-hand side of the graph is the FANG weighting in 2020. As you can see, in 2020 five stocks accounted for 21.5% of S&P 500 market cap. These were Microsoft, Apple, Amazon, Alphabet (Google), and Facebook.

Then, in the tables following the chart, we see how the Nifty Fifty and the Tech Stocks dramatically sold off for the next five-year and even ten-year periods. In the third table, we show the five most concentrated stocks of the FANG period with their P/E multiples. We have yet to see how this period will play out.

Concentration of S&P 500 Market Cap in the Index's Five Largest Stocks

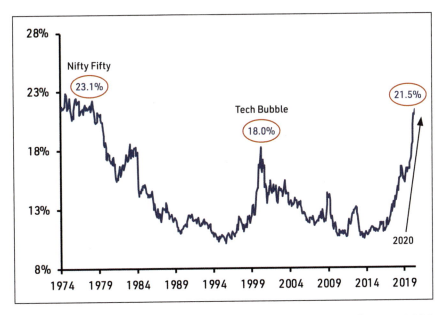

Source: *Morgan Stanley Research, June 2020.*

Growth Stock Corrections

The Nifty Fifty Bubble of 1973–1975

Major Expansion	Top Stocks	P/E Multiple at Peak	Return 5 Years Later (1980)	Return 10 Years Later (1985)
Nifty Fifty				
	Avon Products	63x	−58%	−66%
	Xerox	254x	−70%	−83%
	Polaroid	26x	−79%	−87%
	Eastman Kodak	24x	−66%	−42%

The Tech Bubble of 2000

Major Expansion	Top Stocks	P/E Multiple at Peak	Return 5 Years Later (2005)	Return 10 Years Later (2010)
Tech Bubble				
	Cisco	230x	−78%	−67%
	Intel	50x	−66%	−76%
	Microsoft	79x	−55%	−48%
	Oracle	60x	−71%	−41%

The FANG Bubble of 2020

Major Expansion	Top Stocks	P/E Multiple (6/30/2020)	Return 5 Years Later (2025)	Return 10 Years Later (2030)
FANG				
	Facebook	52x	?	?
	Amazon	243x	?	?
	Netflix	471x	?	?
	Google	38x	?	?

Source: SCCM, 2021 For illustrative purposes only.
This is not a recommendation to buy or sell the stocks shown.

7

—

Risk-Adjusted
Performance

O NE OF THE biggest risks for an investor is ignoring risk. The financial industry has always used absolute performance as a way to measure how well a portfolio manager is doing. This seems logical, but it is one reason why so many investors find themselves paying up for stocks when they are high and selling out when they are low.

The traditional tool for evaluating the performance of portfolio managers is to look at their absolute performance numbers over one-, three- and five-year periods. The temptation is to keep the best five-year performers and fire the worst. While that would seem to make sense, history shows that, often, just the opposite should be done because many times investors are taking too much risk to chase performance.

If this is the case, how does one deal with the situation? One answer is to look at performance on a risk-adjusted basis.

In Wall Street sales literature, there is always a lot of talk about risk, but it never seems to get linked to a performance measurement. The average investor wants absolute performance, but he should want risk to be part of the consideration—and risk can be measured.

There are two basic, easy to understand and generally accepted standard measurements of risk used by financial analysts. One is beta, which is the volatility of an individual stock, and the other is standard deviation, which is the volatility of a portfolio overall. In the following study, a unit of performance is adjusted for an equal part of risk. To illustrate how the measurement plays out, I use the example of the Schafer Cullen High Dividend composite.

The following chart tracks the last nine-year period when value has been out of favor. During that time, the Schafer Cullen High Dividend performance was +14.8%, versus +17.3% for the Russell 1000 Value and +18.2% for the S&P 500. However, when measured on a risk-adjusted basis, one gets a completely different picture. The Schafer Cullen High Dividend portfolio outperformed the S&P 500 by almost 200 basis points and the Russell 1000 by 300 basis points over this same period on a risk-adjusted basis.

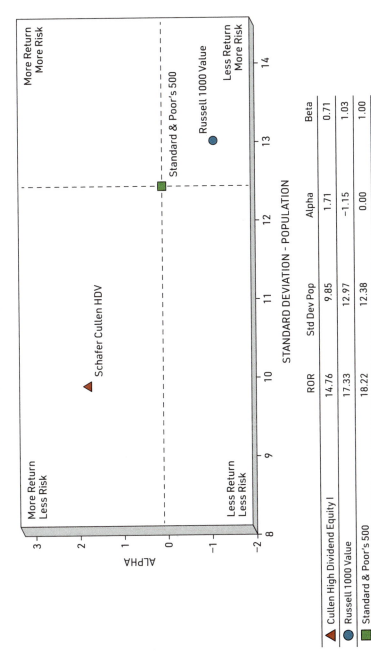

Risk-Adjusted Alpha: February 28, 2009 To December 31, 2017

STANDARD DEVIATION - POPULATION

ALPHA

	ROR	Std Dev Pop	Alpha	Beta
▲ Cullen High Dividend Equity I	14.76	9.85	1.71	0.71
● Russell 1000 Value	17.33	12.97	-1.15	1.03
■ Standard & Poor's 500	18.22	12.38	0.00	1.00

Risk benchmark used for this analysis: Standard & Poor's 500.

In conclusion, regarding risk, an investor should be sure that they or whoever they are working with is including some measure of risk when looking at investment performance.

8

—

Long-Term Value—
A Summary

It Works!

THE FOLLOWING TABLE is the best way to summarize the advantage of a value investment strategy, which includes rolling five-year returns, value vs. the index (passive), recessions, and bear markets.

Long-Term Investing, Active vs. Passive, Consecutive Five-Year Periods (1968–2017)

	Bottom 20% Stocks by P/E Return	S&P 500 (Passive) Return	Recessions	Bear Markets	Bear Market Drop
1968–1972	8.0%	7.5%	1969–1970	2/1968–5/1970	−36%
1973–1977	14.2%	−0.2%	1974–1975	1/1973–2/1974	−46%
1978–1982	24.4%	14.1%	1979 / 1981–1982	4/1981–8/1982	−24%
1983–1987	20.1%	16.5%		8/1987–10/1987	−33%
1988–1992	18.1%	15.1%	1990–1991	7/1990–10/1990	−20%
1993–1997	22.5%	20.3%			
1998–2002	7.0%	−0.6%	2000–2001	7/1998–8/1998	−19%
				1/2000–9/2001	−34%
				3/2002–10/2002	−34%
2003–2007	18.2%	12.8%		10/2007–3/2009	−56%
2008–2012	5.6%	1.7%	2008–2010	4/2011–10/2011	−19%
2013–2017	17.6%	15.8%			
2018–2022	-	-	-	-	-
Annualized Average:	**15.4%**	**10.1%**			
1968–2017 ($1 million)	$1,281 million	$120 million			

*Annualized Returns.
Source: SCCM Research, 2018.*

The data in the table demonstrates the advantage of a value discipline and the use of rolling five-year periods to measure performance.

Column one covers all the five-year investment periods for the bottom 20% of the S&P 500 by P/E. Column two repeats the exercise for the S&P 500, which is the equivalent of passive or index performance.

Columns three and four show the recessions and bear markets in each of the five-year periods. Column five shows the percentage drop in the market during those bear markets.

The results of the study are that the average annualized return of the bottom 20% of stocks by P/E was 15%, while the average annualized return of the S&P 500 was 10%. The return for growth (top 20% by P/E) was 9.7%. The bottom line of the table shows the total value of a million dollars invested in each strategy starting in 1968 and ending in 2017.

For new investors, the real challenge is to get through the five-year cycle. At some point in the first five years there will be a time when they will say, "Why am I in the market?" or, "Why am I in value?" Or both.

In most cases, we have found that if an investor can get through that first five-year period, this helps them to become believers in the long-term value approach to investing and helps them to stay the course.

Staying the course

After reviewing the 100-year history of the market in Section One, where we looked at the 100-year battle for investors, you can appreciate how hard it is to stick with an investment strategy through thick and thin.

The following is an example of what can happen if one stays the course.

Florida MDs

When I was at Donaldson, Lufkin and Jenrette in the late 1970s and early 1980s, I was managing money for some doctors in the Palm Beach, Florida area. IRA accounts were a new vehicle at the time, enabling investors to put away small amounts of money, tax free, each year.

The doctors contributed to their IRAs each year, but didn't pay much attention to the trivial amounts of money in the accounts. Instead, they focused their time on their practices, investing in real estate, fancy cars, second wives, and so on. After a few years, some of these accounts were getting large enough so the doctors started to notice them. One of the senior doctors, who was a highly respected physician and investor, kept encouraging his fellow practitioners not to touch their IRA accounts.

Fifty years later I still manage money for a few of the MDs and their IRA accounts. Because they have stayed invested, their accounts are up as much as 6,000% since inception and are now worth tens of millions of dollars, even while in many cases millions of dollars had been withdrawn. Meanwhile, most of the doctors' other investments did not pan out so well.

The doctors' performance shows the benefits of avoiding all the temptations of market timing schemes over the years.

SECTION THREE

MARKET TIMING

Section Three addresses a subtle but extremely important aspect of successful investing: avoiding market timing. Market timing is the silent killer of long-term performance.

9

Market Timing— The Silent Killer

A MARKET TIMING APPROACH to stocks is exceptionally seductive because investors usually think they are acting for very good reasons. Those reasons, however, still result in a version of, if not the equivalent of, market timing.

Market timing takes two major forms:

1. A strategic shift to cash or cash equivalents.

2. An attempt to improve performance.

Let's look at these in turn.

1. Shifting to Cash

The Experience of Two Investors

Two knowledgeable clients started investing with me on the same day in 1985. One of them, Client A, came to New York once a year to discuss the market and always expressed comfort with our investment approach. Meanwhile, Client B, equally knowledgeable, went into cash, perhaps five times during the course of 20 years, in response to various negative events. For example, Client B went 50% to cash immediately after 9/11, while Client A stayed fully invested.

Twenty years after they started investing, I was curious about the relative performance of the two accounts. I was shocked to learn how just a few moves out of the market could make such a big difference in performance. Client A's performance was 1,000% better than Client B's.

Their 20-year returns were as follows:

- Account A: +1,501%

- Account B: +519%

The Prudential Study

In 1991, Prudential published a study that concluded investors paid a substantial penalty for ill-considered, panicked moves into cash.

Their analysis of returns over 30 years showed that while stocks returned three times more than bonds or the inflation rate over the time span, the advantage was *completely wiped out* if an investor had switched to cash for just 10 key one-month periods of the 360 months during the 30 years.

Obviously, an investor could not know in advance when these key 10 months would be, so it was necessary to stay invested in stocks 100% of the time to get the full benefit of investing in stocks.

Templeton Findings

The legendary global investor, Sir John Templeton, commented at his company's 1992 annual meeting:

> Today, I would say the greatest mistake being made by investors is thinking that they're playing it safe by owning cash. A study that has been ongoing at Templeton Funds for 23 years—from 1969 to 1991—shows that had you been the most fortunate investor and invested in the Templeton Growth Fund at the market low each year, your annual return would have been only 1% higher than had you been unfortunate and invested at the market high each year. So the difference between the best and the worst time to invest is a scant 1%. For long-term investors the message is clear: the best time to invest is when you have the money and forget market timing.

Disaster Scenario

There are times when the experts are so bearish that it is really hard not to go to cash. A perfect example, mentioned earlier in the market history chapter, is the comment from the *Bank Credit Analyst* back in 1981 when it was considered the most highly regarded institutional research firm on Wall Street:

A growing number of individuals and companies are falling behind in their onerous interest payments while the destruction of net worth and incidence of insolvency in the banking industry continues to grow sharply. And all long-lived assets continue to be liquidated—bonds, stocks, commodities and real estate. And this was not likely to stop soon.

The forces creating extreme illiquidity and ultimately deep recession are shaping up quickly: General disaster in the banking area plus extreme financial pressure on states and municipalities and the destruction of key players in the housing sector implies a long recession. The deflationary environment implies a long recession and continued pressure on the weakest sectors of the economy and the worst is yet to come.

This kind of doomsday judgment makes it hard for investors to stay in the market!

When *Bank Credit Analyst's* views were published in October 1981, the economy was still in recession and stocks were at historic lows. At the same time, *Business Week* ran a cover story entitled "The Death of Equities." For long-term investors, that moment proved to be one of the great buying points in history.

This shows that the moments of maximum pessimism are not moments to go to cash or switch to other "safer" assets. This kind of market timing is a killer of investment performance.

Dow Jones Industrial Average (1975–2005)

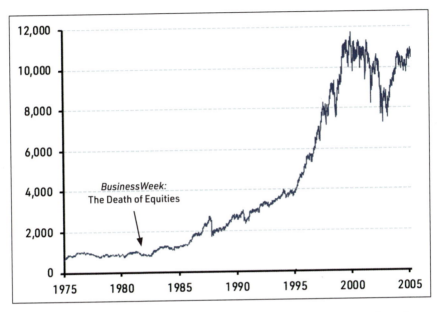

Source: Bloomberg.

2. Improving Performance

Peter Lynch on Market Timing

During the 1980s and 1990s, Peter Lynch managed Fidelity's Magellan Fund, the largest and most popular mutual fund in the country. He was regarded as the industry's top mutual fund manager. Magellan was up on average 15% every year for 15 years. Lynch's comments on market timing were as follows:

> Trying to predict what the Dow is going to do a year from now or six months from now is useless. It's amazing to me how much time people spend trying to predict the stock market. If you spend over 14 minutes a year on economics, you've wasted 12 minutes.

From one year to the next, the stock market is a coin flip; it can go up or down. The real money in stocks is made in the third, fourth and fifth year of your investment because you are participating in a company's earnings, which grow over time.

Regarding Lynch and market timing, there was a story around for years about a Fidelity study, which concluded that despite the phenomenal performance of Lynch's fund, most investors in the fund did not make money and many actually lost money. The reason: many investors bought the fund when the news was good and the fund price was high, and would bail out when the news was bad and the fund price was down.

Fidelity has denied the existence of the study, but there is probably some truth to what Magellan investors reportedly experienced.

Investor's Intelligence Study

Investor's Intelligence provides a survey of stock market letter writers, going back many years. At the beginning of 1995, the start of one of the strongest five-year periods in market history, an all-time record 60% of the letter writers polled were bearish. At the time, these presumed experts seemed to have plenty of good reasons for their bearishness. But what followed was one of the strongest five-year periods in history: 1995–2000.

Tactical Asset Allocation

In the late 1980s, my firm started managing money for a large state pension fund. The fund's investment committee was very risk averse and was comfortable with the value strategy.

Six months after their investment began, the market was up and the performance was very good. However, the pension fund called and said that while they were impressed with the results, they had an opportunity which seemed too good to turn down, so they were going to transfer the account to a firm in San Francisco, which had developed this new strategy.

What they couldn't resist was a new strategy called *Tactical Asset Allocation*. It was based on a so-called proprietary formula (today it would be called an algorithm), which would give a supposedly perfect signal of when to be in equities and when to be in bonds.

At the time, the Tactical Asset Allocation strategy was just becoming the rage of the pension fund business and a couple of San Francisco firms were raising billions using it.

Once the new firm started managing the pension fund's assets, they got a signal to get out of stocks and into bonds, which they did. The market, which had been going higher, continued to move up after the switch. As the market climbed even higher, the manager started to feel pressure from clients who complained they were out of stocks in the middle of a strong bull market. The manager, reacting to the pressure, tweaked the formula, enabling them to move back into stocks.

It turned out the shift marked the top of the stock market, leading to a major sell-off. Six months later, clients were bailing out of the Tactical Asset Allocation strategy and it hasn't been heard of since.

However, while the term Tactical Asset Allocation is long gone, variations on the approach, algorithmic strategies among them, are being offered to clients all the time, usually with the same negative results.

Summary

This survey of the two types of market timing—switching out of stocks into cash or to other assets in an attempt to improve performance—has shown that market timing is truly a silent killer of investment performance.

SECTION FOUR

PICKING
THE STOCKS

This is where we translate the theory of long-term value into practice, by picking stocks in which to invest.

10

Research Process

THE FIRST PART of stock picking is research. The investor needs to find stocks in which to invest.

There is a huge universe of stocks from which to choose and the research process helps the investor to winnow down that universe into a smaller number of stocks to research further, and then an even smaller number of stocks to add to the portfolio.

When starting with a new portfolio, a good number of stocks to have in a portfolio for adequate diversification is 30–35, generally equally weighted, with no more than 15% of the portfolio allocated to any one industry, to avoid concentration risk.

The investment process starts by running screens to come up with companies to analyze further. The universes screened include the S&P 500, Russell Indexes, Value Line, various international indexes, and others.

This chapter reviews some of the various statistical measures used to screen stocks, of course starting with the three major investment disciplines: price-to-earnings, price-to-book, and dividend yield.

Price/Earnings Multiple

P/E multiples historically have swung from lows of roughly 10x earnings to highs of 20x+ earnings over time. The interest is not the absolute level of P/E multiple, but rather investing in stocks that are selling at a 20–50% discount to the P/E of the overall market (S&P 500). When a stock appreciates to where its P/E multiple exceeds the market average, the stock becomes a candidate for eventual sale and replacement in the portfolio.

Price/Book

We saw in the original study of the disciplines in Section Two that the historical performance of Price/Book is very competitive with dividend yield and Price/Earnings. This is surprising in that today, book value is not used as much because many stocks—in industries like technology, healthcare and consumer products—sell at a very high price relative to their book. For this reason, P/B is more important for certain industries like airlines and metals. In general, for those industries, stocks selling at 2x book or less are preferred.

Dividend Yield

For strategies where it is a primary focus, a yield of 3% or higher at inception is the goal. If because of market appreciation the yield gets down below 2%, replacing the stock in the portfolio with a higher-yielding stock becomes the objective.

Dividend Growth

Not only is dividend yield important, but dividend growth is also important for long-term performance. Ideally one likes to see stocks growing their dividend in the high single digits to 10% level.

Dividend Payout Ratio

There is a preference to see the payout ratio generally not much higher than 50%. When a company is struggling and paying out too big of a percentage of earnings in dividends, it is a signal that dividend growth could slow or maybe even be cut.

Debt-Equity-Ratio

The debt-equity-ratio is especially important when a company runs into tough economic times. Companies that have a debt/equity ratio of less than 50% are generally preferred. While debt tends to get ignored in up markets, when a recession or major bear market hits the most leveraged companies often get wiped out.

Debt Coverage

How much debt a company has is important, but it's equally important to observe how much cash the company is generating relative to its total outstanding debt and its ability to meet its interest obligations. Debt service coverage of 3x or higher is attractive.

Return on Capital

Return on capital is a percentage showing how fast a company is growing its business. As a rule, one likes to see a company with a 10% return on capital. Little attention is paid to return on equity since that ratio depends on leverage and is used more by investment bankers.

Current Ratio

Current ratio is the ratio of current assets to current liabilities and is used as a guide to the balance sheet strength of a company and its ability to meet its short-term obligations. Historically, a 2:1 ratio of current assets to current liabilities is a sign that a company is financially strong.

While statistical analysis is important, it is just the start of the research process. It's also important for the investor to have ideas about where to find good stocks.

In the rest of Section Four we will look at where the best stock picking ideas have come from over the years. As you will see, they came from very diverse places.

11

Book Value

AS DISCUSSED EARLIER, Book Value was one of Ben Graham's recommended price disciplines, along with Price/Earnings and Dividend Yield. While the primary interest is always in P/E, screening for book value is important for some industries.

When looking at companies in certain sectors of the market, book value is a more reliable measure of a stock's appeal than P/E. Examples would be cyclical companies like airlines, metals, energy, and other commodity stocks.

A company's book value, defined as its assets minus liabilities, is a rough approximation of its liquidation value. While accounting principles tend to be conservative in terms of how assets are priced, companies and their financial officers, and outside accountants, have considerable leeway in valuing a firm's assets. So an investor has to comb through the financial statements and determine what a company's assets are actually worth and what its liabilities actually are.

A powerful brand like Coca-Cola is hard to evaluate, as is valuing the intellectual property of a tech company or an important drug for a pharmaceutical company. Today, because most companies are not in manufacturing but offer some kind of service, book value no longer occupies the place it once did among financial analysts.

But despite the dominance of the tech era, with its high price-to-book ratios, a low price-to-book can still have value. Surprisingly, a review of the returns of the value disciplines over the long term and even over more recent periods (see Chapter 2) shows that price-to-book has provided very competitive performance to that of P/E and dividend yield.

Of course, there is always the danger of mispricing assets. Investors learned this the hard way in the case of large US bank stocks during the Financial Crisis of 2008. Wall Street analysts were recommending the stocks because they were selling at attractive prices relative to book value. But the derivative securities in their portfolios were hugely overpriced and when they came to be correctly priced, banks like Lehman Brothers, Bear Sterns, and AIG were wiped out. So you always have to be careful analyzing book value—and the same goes for earnings in this new era of creative accounting.

An example of how analysis of book value can be used in the research process can be seen in the example of De Beers.

De Beers

The British company De Beers operated one of the largest diamond mining companies in the world. The bulk of their assets were in South Africa. At the time it seemed to be attractively priced at $15/share, selling at roughly book value and at 10x earnings with a 5% dividend yield. Moreover, five investment firms were following the company and all had "strong buy" recommendations on the stock.

What was not to like?

A lot actually, as bad news about the company's market environment emerged. First the Russians, who were having financial problems at the time, started dumping diamonds on the world market. Then it was announced that there was a massive diamond find in Canada, which was also going to have a major impact on supply. The combination of the two put pressure on De Beers' stock price. The coup de gras was a story on the widely watched *60 Minutes* news show, which reported South African mine workers stealing diamonds from De Beers and other companies.

The events combined to produce a 33% drop in the stock price to $10/share. To make matters worse, all five investment firms that had strong buys on the stock changed their recommendations to outright sell. This left my firm Schafer Cullen out in the cold, with no outside research support.

One of the most important tasks in the research process, as pointed out in Chapter 13, is to make "a call away from Wall Street" to get a different slant on a company's business. In the case of De Beers, I organized a call to the Oppenheimer family, the company's largest shareholder. They said they were not selling the stock at the present time, but neither were they buying. Because the family wasn't selling and because the valuations were so attractive, I decided to hold the position.

Meanwhile, the stock drifted a bit lower and dropped under $10/share. It was now selling at 5x earnings, the yield climbed to about 8%, and the company still had no debt. While it wasn't clear how much earnings might be impacted by the negative news, the stock was now selling at half of book value, and book value was comprised of diamonds.

Clients were panicking, but because of the company's attractive valuations, it paid not to sell. Three months later, the Oppenheimer family stepped up and bought all the stock at $35/share. What saved the investment was not only the company's cheap valuation, but also making the call away to the Oppenheimer family to get that outside view.

12

Have a Story

EVALUATING THE FINANCIAL fundamentals of a company is very important in stock selection, but it's just the start of the research process.

The next step is to look for a company where there is something to get excited about. Maybe it's new management, or a new product, or new markets.

In short, one is looking for companies that are cheap on a valuation basis and have a story that will result in a higher stock price. Following are some examples.

PetroChina

Back in 2001 I went to a breakfast hosted by Kurt H. Wulff, then at Donaldson, Lufkin & Jenrette. I had once worked with him at DLJ and was impressed with his research skills. Kurt was one of Wall Street's leading oil analysts and ranked by *Institutional Investor* magazine year after year as one of the Street's best.

That morning he made a presentation about the overall outlook for the energy sector. Near the end of his remarks, he made a case for a couple of international stocks, PetroChina and CNOOC, which were new to his coverage. He believed them attractive because they were dramatically cheaper than comparable US and European oil stocks.

Both companies were backed by the Chinese government, which raised some concerns. But Kurt's research led him to believe the Chinese wanted very much to introduce a few of their major companies as examples of the potential for their economy.

PetroChina was the largest domestic oil company in China and had the largest oil reserves in the country. China was a country with huge environmental problems because 90% of its energy came from coal. With oil being a much cleaner fuel than coal, PetroChina was part of the solution. The company also had huge untapped natural gas resources in western China, and gas was even cleaner than oil.

The stock was purchased at the end of 2001 and five years later it was up 700%, as investment in Chinese companies in general became more acceptable in the global marketplace.

PetroChina (2000–2007)

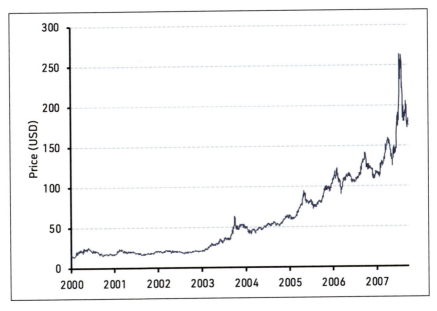

Source: Bloomberg.

Diageo

The entire consumer staples sector had been out of favor since the 1990s. The sector was considered mature and its prospects for growth limited. The first stock from this group that was researched and eventually purchased was Diageo. Later, Unilever and Kimberly-Clark were bought from the staples sector.

Diageo first came to my attention when a colleague went to a Chinese wedding and noticed they had Johnnie Walker instead of champagne on the tables. Looking for a way to invest in the Chinese market, maybe the huge growth potential of the wedding business was not a bad place to start.

Diageo was selling at a low P/E multiple of 10x and had a relatively high dividend yield of 4%. The company's earnings report showed that growth in emerging market sales was four or five times the growth rate of the rest of the company. However, since the emerging market sales represented only 5% of total sales, it did not get much attention from the Wall Street analysts.

The belief was that eventually the growth in this small segment of the business was going to dramatically drive earnings.

A concern in doing business in emerging markets is the possibility of a government creating copycat products. However, having strong brand names like Johnnie Walker and Guinness, Diageo was probably not going to have that problem.

Over the next five years, Diageo saw their emerging markets revenues grow from 5% to roughly 50%, resulting in Diageo's P/E multiple going from 10x to 20x, and the stock price going up 350%.

Diageo (2004–2021)

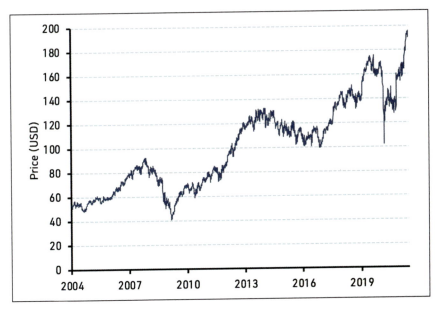

Disney

Disney is a story for investors in many different ways.

First, it could be recognised as having extraordinary management, since Bob Iger, its former CEO, is credited as being one of the best CEOs in the US.

Also, Disney has created a world-class entertainment lineup through its creation of Disney movies and its purchase of the Pixar entertainment division, not to mention ESPN sports and theme parks. Some of Disney's businesses are cyclical, which provided investors with the opportunity to buy the stock at various times at relatively attractive prices.

The story that remains to be fully realized going forward is the opening of the Disney theme park in Shanghai. Unlike Euro-Disney, which was not well marketed and never very successful, the experience for Disney in Shanghai has been extremely positive. It opened in 2016 with 11 million visitors the first year and was on track to be a runaway success.

13D Research analyst Kiril Sokoloff, who over the years has come up with some fascinating ideas, pointed out that young students in China very much want to learn English. Disney set up language instruction classes using Disney characters in after-school programs. Initially 150 programs were set up. A year later, there were 1,500.

The after-school programs were a great and subtle way to get exposure to the Chinese market. That Chinese children are learning the English language from Disney characters should also help bring Chinese families to Disney theme parks, lead them to see Disney films and encourage them to buy Disney products.

Disney (2006–2021)

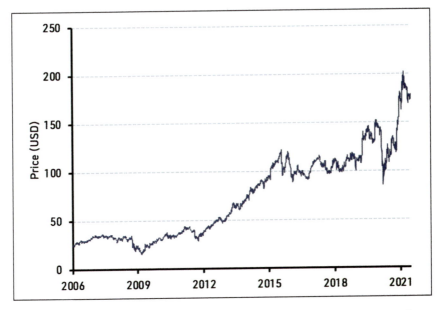

Source: Bloomberg.

Unilever

Another consumer staple stock purchased in 2007 was Unilever. Unilever is highlighted later in this section ("The Three-Point Fix")— and other staple stocks like Diageo and Kimberly-Clark could have been included there too—but Unilever is included here for the purpose of its story.

What first got my attention about Unilever was an article in the *Financial Times* which reported that Unilever, an Anglo-Dutch company, had been in Indonesia for over 100 years. This of course would give Unilever a big edge in the international markets over an American company like Proctor & Gamble. Because of the company's attractive valuation and strong international and emerging market business, the stock was purchased.

At that time I was being interviewed on Bloomberg TV and was asked for my three favorite stocks. Unilever was mentioned as one of the three and when asked why, I pointed out the stock was very oversold and valuations were very attractive because the research community had been saying Unilever's products and management were boring. However, I felt that the company's emerging markets exposure would eventually play out.

When I got back to the office following the TV interview, I got a call from Unilever's head of marketing. He said he watched the interview and would like his "boring" management team to come to our offices and show us the company's "boring" products.

A week later, the management team showed up for a 9:00 am meeting with an array of products, which they set up in the conference room. I looked at products including Dove soap, Lipton Tea, and other similarly familiar, old brands and thought "these products actually do look a bit boring, or at least passé."

The Unilever team made a presentation lasting four hours. All the analysts and portfolio managers were in attendance and were left speechless by management's explanation of how they were developing individualized products for specific markets and the rationale behind the marketing of each product.

One example was Dove soap. They showed how in the US, a huge box of detergent is the most popular because it is cheaper, but in a place like Indonesia, the woman doing the wash often has to walk a mile to a washing machine. For her, a six pack of small soaps makes more sense.

Another example came from our portfolio manager, Jennifer Chang, who visited China a few weeks later. She learned that Lipton Tea, which we all regarded as yesterday's tea, was very popular in China where Lipton had created a cold tea juice box product catering to the Chinese taste. It became a huge seller.

Over the last several years, Unilever's emerging markets sales have grown from 5% of their business to over 50% and the stock price has benefitted accordingly.

Unilever (2005–2021)

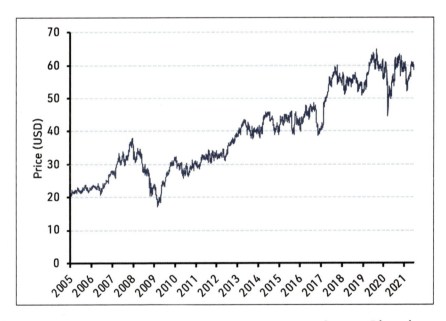

Source: Bloomberg.

13

Making a Call Away
from Wall Street

A N OFTEN OVERLOOKED but extremely important part of
the research process is making a call away from Wall Street.
The objective is to get another view of a company.

A major problem converting an investment strategy into a portfolio
of stocks is sorting through the blizzard of information. Most of the
information is helpful, but not everything we read or hear, of course,
can be trusted. Some information misleads and some shows evidence
of conflict of interest. So we need to be careful. United Defense
Industries is an example of how to deal with what appeared to be
credible information.

United Defense Industries

It was 1985 and military spending had been in decline for a decade. However, tensions in the Middle East were growing and it looked like Congress was going to increase defense spending. Therefore, it made sense to add to the defensive holdings.

Coincidentally, two major Wall Street research firms came out with strong buy reports on a company I had never heard of—United Defense Industries. The research reports said the stock was selling at an attractive 10x earnings and was a pure defense play.

Also, a strong case was made for the company's main product: a huge tank called the Crusader, which seemed perfect for Middle East combat. The tank accounted for more than half the company's earnings. There were reports the Crusader had more firepower than the F-11 fighter plane. It looked like a stock with a story!

Reading the research reports, it turned out that UDI only had a six-month history. It was a new issue and the first ever offering from the private equity firm Carlyle.

Also, the two *strong buy* reports came from the same two firms which were UDI's investment bankers. Research and brokerage operations are legally restricted from doing reports on their firm's banking clients for six months after an offering. The six months had expired, but because brokerage firms receive major fees from their investment banking relationships, a red flag went up indicating a possible conflict of interest.

Also worrisome, Carlyle was then a new and little-known private equity firm, making its first offering. In general, it has paid to be leery of buying a stock being spun out by private equity firms. They tend to load spin-outs with a lot of debt. Such was the case with UDI.

Despite everything, the company was still intriguing because of its valuation and the Crusader. As part of the research process, some calls were made away from Wall Street.

It turned out Carlyle was put together by a group of Washington insiders, who specialized in defense companies. One of the insiders and a founder of the firm was the highly regarded former Secretary of Defense, Frank Carlucci.

Because of the large amount of debt and the brokerage firms' possible conflict of interest, it made sense to make a few more calls. The next one was to Paul Nisbet, a highly regarded defense analyst from First Boston. He was a regular all-star selected by *Institutional Investor* magazine. He had provided a lot of great advice in the past and was now an independent consultant.

I asked Paul about UDI's huge debt and the little-known private equity firm and he said I was probably worrying about the wrong things. The real worry was the Crusader. He thought it was too big and unwieldy for practical battlefield use and the tank program could easily be shelved.

After talking with Nisbet, I called one of the two investment banking firms and passed along Nisbet's concerns. The research analyst said big defense contracts were pork barrel projects of members of Congress and seldom cut.

There were enough doubts about the company, so I decided to hold off any purchase. A month later, by pure coincidence, I was watching Senate confirmation hearings for Donald Rumsfeld as Secretary of Defense. At that point in his career, he was an extremely popular choice and the senators did nothing but try to flatter him. Rumsfeld, taking advantage of his position, warned the politicians that if he took the job, he would not hesitate to cut pet programs that he thought were a waste of money.

No more thought was given to UDI, but about a month later, Rumsfeld, as the Secretary of Defense, held a press conference announcing cancellation of the Crusader program. The stock, which had been selling around $30/share, dropped approximately 50%.

I called Nisbet and thanked him for steering me away from a bad decision. He said he appreciated hearing from me, and then said "by the way," one of the same investment banking firms was planning another new issue he thought worth looking into. This was a Navy ship building company with huge cash flows and was also being spun out by Carlyle. Nisbet said that because of a bad start with UDI, Carlyle would probably price the new company attractively.

I once again called one of the same investment banking firms and said I was interested in the new offering. They told me the deal was cancelled and UDI was buying the new company. Carlyle apparently decided that putting the two companies together would salvage their reputation from the bad UDI experience.

I immediately called Paul Nisbet again, and told him what was happening. He said that the new company should be very interesting because the Navy ship building company's cash flow would address a lot of UDI's debt problems. Also, the Crusader tank would probably be scaled down to become a more practical vehicle. Armed with Nisbet's analysis, the stock was purchased at roughly $20/share. Three years later, the company was taken over by BAE Systems for $75/share, up 250%.

If the "call away" to Paul Nisbet had not been made and one had relied only on the brokerage house research reports, the stock would have probably been bought at $30/share, and then when the stock dropped to $20/share on the Crusader news, one might have easily been tempted or pressured to sell it. History shows that when you buy bad, you usually wind up selling bad. A few extra phone calls away from Wall Street prevented buying too early and ended up with a successful investment.

14

Management

EVALUATING A COMPANY'S management can be a very important part of the research process. Of course, the larger the company the harder it is in most cases to get a feel for the strength of its top management. But getting that feel is sometimes the most important consideration in stock selection.

Some of the questions to ask in trying to evaluate top managers are: how much stock do they own in the company; how enthusiastic are they about the company's prospects; and is management up to the job?

Following are a couple of examples where a judgment about the strength of management was the principal reason for buying the stock.

Jamie Dimon and JP Morgan

Early in his career, Jamie Dimon worked under Sandy Weil at American Express and Citigroup, but left over some nebulous management conflict. Dimon was one of the most popular executives at these firms and people really liked working for him.

In 2000, Dimon took the top job at Chicago's Bank One where he was a great success. In July of 2004, Bank One was acquired by JP Morgan. The timing was good and it gave Morgan a bit of a lift.

The reason for buying the stock was Dimon going to JP Morgan. Early reports were everybody at Morgan was very happy with his leadership and banking employees on Wall Street all seemed to want to work for Jamie Dimon.

The following chart shows how JP Morgan's stock has performed since Dimon became CEO. Earnings and dividends have grown steadily and the Jamie Dimon-led JP Morgan has become the star of the financial stocks.

JP Morgan (2000–2021)

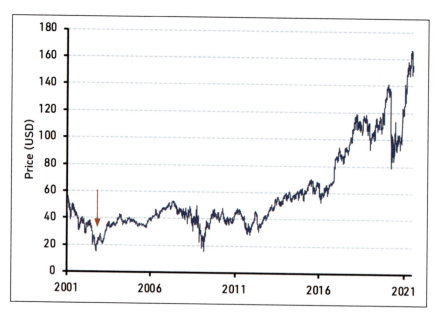

Source: Bloomberg.

Mark Hurd and Hewlett-Packard

During the 1970s and 1980s, Hewlett-Packard was a leading technology company. In 2002, HP acquired Compaq Computer, a major acquisition. History shows that large acquisitions usually don't work out and this was the case here.

When it was announced in 2005 that Mark Hurd was to become CEO, Hewlett-Packard's stock was depressed, with earnings weighed down by the Compaq acquisition. Mark Hurd's success at National Cash Register, where he developed a reputation for turning around a troubled company, was a reason to buy the stock. When Hurd took the reins at HP, the Compaq acquisition was three years in the past, and it seemed the time was right for the company to start doing better under the right manager.

Mark Hurd turned out to be that manager, as a very good cost-cutter and a great communicator. Both skills, among others, were ultimately reflected in a higher stock price, as you can see from the following chart.

Hewlett-Packard (2005–2010)

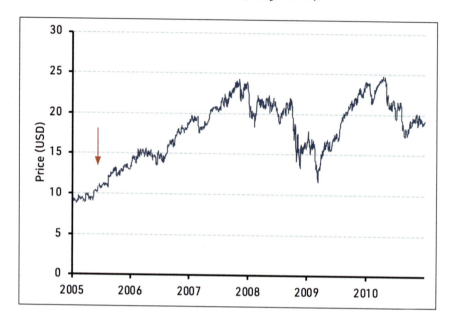

Source: Bloomberg.

Sir John Egan and Jaguar

Jaguar is the British car manufacturer spun out from British Leyland in 1984. While everyone loved the image of the car, there was not a whole lot of interest in the stock because the company had a horrible reputation owing to the car's unreliability. The joke was that if you owned a Jaguar, you really had to have two, because one was always in the shop.

Our firm became interested in Jaguar's stock because the valuations were at extremely low levels, selling at one-half of book value, and at 5x earnings. The key turned out to be John Egan, the impressive new CEO.

The first thing Egan did was to dramatically increase production, not by spending money to expand the manufacturing facilities, but by adding another shift to work in the existing facilities.

Egan came to New York in 1985 to tell his story. There was very little interest and he wound up having his first meeting in our New York office.

Egan was extremely committed and had a clear vision for the company, realizing that quality had been a major obstacle for a long time. His commitment was a classic example of why spin-offs can be very productive. A stand-alone company can be more effective than one operating inside a larger organization.

The next year when Egan came back to New York, there was a bit more interest in the stock because he did such a good job presenting the story. Meanwhile, progress was being made without dramatically increasing debt.

The quality of the newer cars was starting to improve and interest was developing in the stock. By 1987, with interest in Jaguar growing, Egan's New York meeting was held in the Grand Ballroom of the Waldorf Astoria, accommodating hundreds of investors. Two years later, Ford bought the company for $15/share, up 700% from the original cost.

Jaguar (1984–1989)

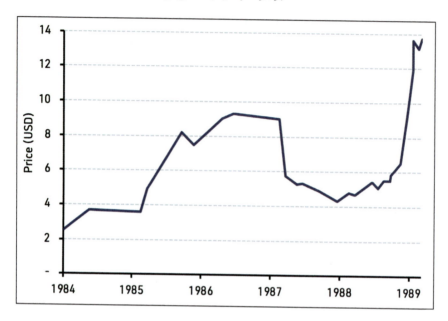

Source: Bloomberg.

15

"By the Way"

SOME OF THE best stock ideas come unexpectedly. Sometimes the surprise comes after a meeting, when someone in an offhand way says: "By the way…" and then says something completely unrelated to the meeting that just took place.

One of the largest percentage gainers in the history of my firm Schafer Cullen came about in just that way. It was 1980, and the research director at the time, Matt Dodds, and I were having lunch with Rudy Mueller, a highly regarded analyst who specialized in metals and defense. We owned International Nickel and Rudy had just come back from visiting the company in Canada and was giving us his view over lunch. Just as we were leaving the restaurant, Rudy said, "By the way, when I was up in Canada, there was talk about the government selling off its nationalized rail companies, Canadian National and Canadian Pacific, both a drain on government finances."

At the time, our recent experience with the US rails had been very positive. After years of sluggish growth, the railroads were aggressively reducing crew sizes, selling off unprofitable spurs, and cutting costs. The result was US rail stocks were reporting stronger earnings and higher stock prices. The favorable experience made us especially interested in what was going on in Canada.

Canadian National

Canadian National was the less profitable of the two and the first the government was spinning out. We looked at the company's initial offering and our interest in the company grew. We became buyers of the stock mainly because of our positive experience with the US rails.

It turned out Canadian National had more upside than the US rails because of CN's long history as a stagnant government company. The earnings and stock price moved up as the company intensified its focus on profitability. The stock was up over 10,000% since the Rudy Mueller lunch.

Canadian National (1995–2021)

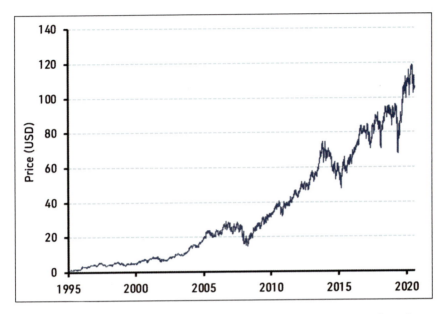

Source: *Bloomberg.*

Canadian Pacific

The results for Canadian Pacific were similar. The company's business was different—more western-oriented and commodities focused—but CP shared the catalyst of a new focus on profitability. The outcomes were pretty much the same.

Canadian Pacific (2001–2021)

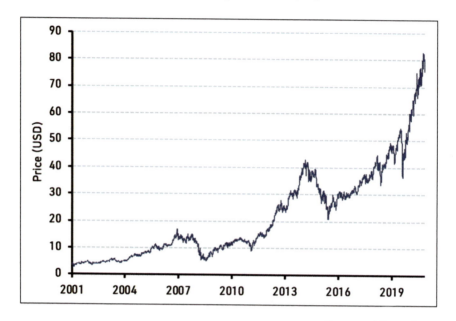

Source: Bloomberg.

16

Insider Buying

INSIDER BUYING BY a company's management is an obvious indication they are enthusiastic about their company's prospects. The assumption is that management believes their company is about to experience growth in sales and earnings.

The job of the investor is to check whether the insider buyers' enthusiasm is justified.

Following are a few examples where insider buying information was an important reason for purchasing the stock.

Citibank—John Reed

Back in 1991, the major New York banks were going through a meltdown because they got caught overweighted in a difficult real estate market. The following chart shows Citibank under pressure and dropping to a record low, at which point co-chairman John Reed stepped up and made a substantial open market purchase of the stock. The chart plainly shows what happened next, as Citi's stock went through a period of strong appreciation.

Citi (1990–1993)

Source: Bloomberg.

JP Morgan—Jamie Dimon

Jamie Dimon, CEO of JP Morgan, provides a second example. He made purchases during the Financial Crisis when Wall Street was worried about a possible meltdown of his investment bank, thanks to its exposure to the highly speculative derivatives market.

Analysts at that time were negative on the entire investment banking industry. In the face of this, Jamie Dimon made a presentation pointing out that the crisis could be handled, and then stepped up and made an $11 million personal purchase of shares after the stock had severely sold off.

In the next chart, you can see how Dimon's confidence was rewarded.

JP Morgan (2004–2017)

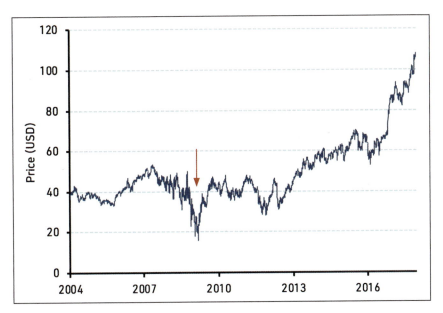

Source: Bloomberg.

Small Cap Stocks

Insider buying is especially interesting in the small cap universe, because managers tend to be close to the companies they run. Also, the stocks are not well followed by Wall Street analysts, thus providing an opportunity. Over the years, this has brought some rewarding investment returns. Following are a couple of examples.

First American National Bank (Tennessee)

In the late 1980s, month after month a number of First American National Bank's directors were buying large blocks of the company's stock. Interestingly, these directors were all close friends and very savvy businessmen so the stock seemed worth researching.

In the 1980s, a major consolidation of the banking industry was taking place in every state. First American was a good example of what was occurring. The company had purchased a couple of very small, inefficient Tennessee banks, and combined them in a roll-up. The managers centralized their banking operations and established a single brand name for the company. While this consolidation increased the size of the bank, we believed it would still be an attractive target for the larger banks. This turned out to be the case. First American was purchased at $10/share and sold a few years later at $25/share.

State O Maine

The Insider Buying Report showed the chairman of State O Maine, David Chu, had started a company called Nautica in 1983, which he sold to State O Maine in 1984. Since then, Chu had been a steady buyer of State O Maine stock.

At the same time, Arnold Blischroder & Company, a very savvy research firm, issued a short, one-paragraph research recommendation. The combination of insider buying and the Blischroder research note led to taking a closer look at the company.

State O Maine was a micro-cap company, had no debt, was selling at a low P/E multiple, and owned a brand called Nautica, which turned out to be the story. Word was that all the crew guys and competitive sailors from Newport, RI loved Nautica products. State O Maine changed its name to Nautica and wound up being one of the top performing stocks in the next decade.

Nautica Enterprises

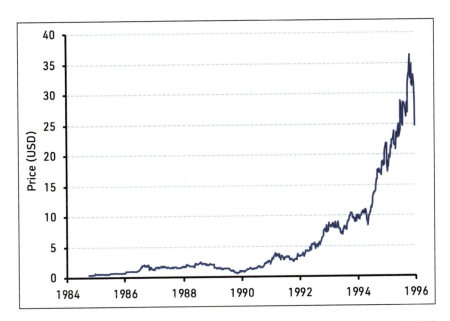

Source: SCCM.

17

Buyer Beware

INVESTORS TODAY HAVE access to high-quality stock research and benefit as well from an SEC that provides regulatory oversight into corporate reporting practices. Overall, the investing environment is much better now than it has been at other times in history. During the 1920s, for example, there was little or no regulation of the stock market and the average investor was the victim.

However, investors today still have to watch out for dangers in unexpected places. Following are a few examples of what has tripped up investors.

Bad Guidance from Analysts

Despite good intentions, research experts can completely miss the reality of what's going on. A classic example featured US bank stocks leading up to the Financial Crisis of 2008. All the Wall Street research firms were aggressively recommending the stocks because they were selling at historically cheap prices relative to book value. There was a catch: because of all the heavy trading the banks were doing, they had taken on a massive amount of derivatives used to hedge their trading.

As the Financial Crisis began to build, the banks' derivative positions had to be liquidated, as it became clear that the positions had reached excessive levels. This meant that the book value of the banks was hugely overstated, thanks to the mispricing of derivatives on their books. Bank stocks collapsed, and old-line names like Lehman Brothers and Bear Stearns went bankrupt, while others, including Citibank and Merrill Lynch, had to be bailed out.

Non-Regulated Investments

Many non-regulated investment vehicles have been useful and popular among experienced, sophisticated investors. But even they can be taken in. An example is the Bernie Madoff scandal.

Madoff had a hedge fund that over the years consistently reported results that appeared too good to be true. After many complaints by investors, the SEC launched a formal investigation, and it turned out the results were literally too good to be true. Madoff's Ponzi scheme was shut down, he went to jail, and his investors lost billions of dollars.

Structured Products

As legendary investor Warren Buffett once said, "If you don't understand it, don't buy it." Today there are many investment products and combinations of products that might work for people wanting to invest, but they shouldn't forget Buffett's advice and make sure they know what they are buying. Many times the problem only becomes obvious after the fact. A classic example is the experience of the Subway Workers Retirement Fund.

The situation occurred during the height of the Covid-19 crisis when the New York subway system was under phenomenal pressure and the Subway Workers Retirement Fund's stated investment objective was to be very risk averse. Even so, a large institutional money manager presented the Fund's board with a so-called "all weather fund." The fund, the manager said, had produced good performance in up-markets, (probably using leverage), and bought and sold options to theoretically protect the fund in down-markets. But in the market correction of the first quarter of 2020, the market sold off and the options didn't do what they were supposed to. The result was that the $330 million pension plan dropped 97% to $9 million.

Be a Contrarian

A lot of historical data shows that presumed experts in stock picking have not had a good track record. There are many cases where the most popular stocks in the beginning of the year underperform the most unpopular stocks by the end of the year. A good example came in January 2010 after the Financial Crisis. A review of the stock picks of analysts at the beginning of 2009 showed the stocks they liked the most were up an average of 73%; while the stocks with the fewest buy recommendations were up double that at 165%.

There are many other examples of the same phenomenon, and they all tend to show the same results. This happens, it has been demonstrated many times, because the most favored stocks tend to get overpriced while the most unpopular stocks represent better value. As Warren Buffett has pointed out, investors pay a high price for popularity.

Performance Trap

A popular way for consultants to analyze and evaluate performance is to look at a money manager's most recent one-, three- and five-year performance results. This can be helpful, but one thing that the results often don't show is the degree of risk taken. In a strong up-market, the best performers' accounts are usually taking the most risk, which might include leverage.

My first experience with risk and leverage happened in my first year at Merrill Lynch when I accompanied a senior broker to a presentation for an established academic foundation. The broker presented five different funds for board members to review. I was sitting next to one of them who said to me, "I see that one of the accounts was up 25% and the rest are a lot lower, why wouldn't we take that one?" And they did. Two years later, the selection proved to be a disaster. It turned out the prior performance of the 25% account was superior because the fund had been highly leveraged and had also invested in the most speculative stocks that benefitted from a bull market. When the market turned down, leverage was the fund's undoing.

Misleading Media

Misleading information can come innocently, even from sources that are the most reliable, like the *Financial Times.*

THE FINANCIAL TIMES
Friday May 24, 2013

Net profits: Ralph Lauren sees leap of 35%

On page one of the May 24, 2013 edition of the *Financial Times*, there was an eye-catching photo of tennis players attired in Polo outfits jumping over a net. The accompanying headline included the words "profits" and "leap." Combined, the photo and the headline may have encouraged investors to go out and buy Ralph Lauren stock.

The reality was a bit different. Buried deep in the paper at the bottom of page 14 was a discussion of the company's earnings outlook, which was less optimistic.

If an investor had bought the stock solely based on the headline and first impression, without reading the full story, three years later he would have lost 50% of his money. This is an example of how it pays to look beyond the headline announcement.

Ralph Lauren (2013–2017)

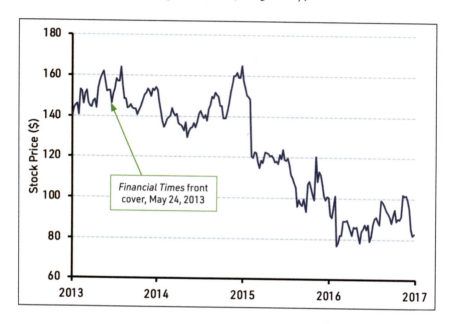

Financial Times front cover, May 24, 2013

Source: Bloomberg.

Summary

The lesson of this chapter is to be careful what you buy and from whom you buy it.

18

When It Doesn't Work

IN MY 50 years in the investment business, one thing has been constant: there is always at least one problem stock in the portfolio, even during the best years. Following are a couple examples.

Diamond Offshore

In January 2013 Diamond Offshore, an oil service company, was selling at $74/share, 11x earnings and with a 6.0% dividend yield. This looked quite interesting, especially when attractively priced stocks with a high dividend yield were hard to find at that time.

Research showed Diamond Offshore had one of the best balance sheets in the oil service business—important because the number of rigs out in the field actually drilling for oil has very volatile swings. A strong balance sheet enables a company to ride out these swings.

There were many favorable research reports on the company and the story was that the company was mostly owned and controlled by the Tisch family. Larry Tisch, the head of the family, had a great reputation as a value investor who loved dividends.

I called Kurt Wulff, the highly regarded Donaldson, Lufkin and Jenrette analyst mentioned earlier. Kurt said he didn't follow the oil service stocks because they were too volatile and behaved more like trading vehicles than stocks for investment.

Ignoring Kurt's advice, the stock was bought because of the combination of high yield, attractive valuation, strong balance sheet, and reputation of the Tisch family. As it turned out, I should have listened to Kurt Wulff. The lesson demonstrated the danger of overreaching for yield.

The oil rig glut was worse than expected. Also, some of Diamond's non-energy, less-visible businesses were having problems. The stock was sold at $17/share. The shares continued to go down to $1/share.

Allied Capital

Here again was a mistake of reaching for yield. Allied Capital, a financial services company, in 2002 was selling in the mid-20 dollars per share, at 10x earnings with a dividend of 6%. The stock was also strongly recommended by many Wall Street firms.

However, financial services companies like Allied were a lot more complicated than most people thought.

As the Financial Crisis unfolded, it turned out Allied was just the tip of the iceberg and many financial companies were getting involved with very questionable creative accounting, which became obvious in the market's financial meltdown. The stock was sold for a tax loss in December 2008 at $2/share, on its way to Chapter 11.

Summary

I have learned over the years that the incentive for companies to grow their earnings sometimes becomes irresistible, so much so that management occasionally pushes the limits. Thus, making that extra call, doing the extra due diligence, studying the balance sheet and assessing management are crucial aspects of the stock selection research process. Even then things can slip by.

19

The Three-Point Fix

THE IDEA FOR the three-point fix goes back to my days in the Navy aboard the aircraft carrier USS *Essex*. If the ship was fogged in while trying to enter the harbor, the chances for success were good in navigational terms if you had one navigational fix—like the bearings off of a lighthouse. If you could get a second fix—like a flashing buoy—that dramatically increased your chances of being successful. If you had a third fix, that would virtually guarantee your success, even in the worst fog conditions.

In stock market terms, a stock with attractive valuations, like a low P/E, is the equivalent of having one navigational fix, which alone would provide a good chance of investment success. An example of a second fix is having a strong story, which would dramatically improve your chances of being successful.

The key third navigational fix has two parts. First, the stock is oversold relative to the S&P 500. Second, momentum for the stock is starting to turn up. Adding this third fix has resulted in the best stock returns over time.

Let's look at three examples of the Three-Point Fix in Unilever, Disney, and Microsoft.

Unilever

We have already discussed Unilever in Chapter 12, "Have a Story." For Unilever, the *first fix* was the company's attractive valuation. The stock was selling at 10x earnings with a 4% dividend yield.

The *second fix* was the story, which as we discussed earlier, was the potential explosive growth in the emerging markets.

The key part I of the *third fix* was the stock being out of favor because it was considered a stodgy, slow-growth company. Chart 1 shows how the stock was out of favor in 2004. Part II of the third fix can be seen in chart 2, where momentum is starting to turn up.

Unilever: Chart 1 (Third Fix Part I—Out of Favor)

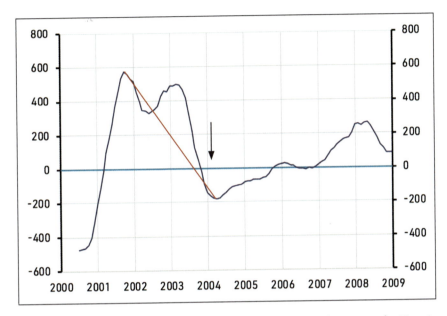

Momentum chart showing rate of change relative to the Y axis.

Chart 2 shows how momentum was starting to pick up for the stock. The combination of parts 1 and 2 of the third fix.

Unilever: Chart 2 (Third Fix Part II—Momentum)

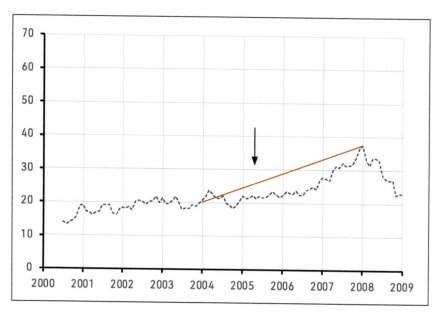

Momentum chart showing Stock Price / S&P 500.

Chart 3 shows the results.

Unilever: Chart 3—Results

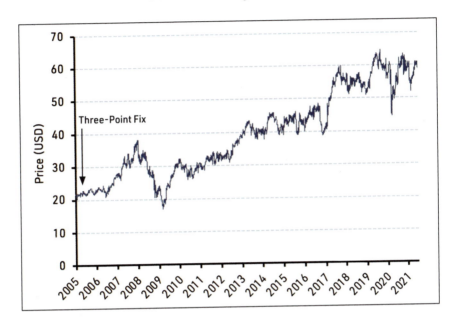

Disney

Back in 2004–2005, Disney stock was down to an attractive P/E level because of disappointing growth in its parks and entertainment businesses. At the same time, management seemed to be in disarray, resulting in the valuation being very attractive at 11x earnings (*first fix*).

Then came the story: a change in management. Eisner was rumored to be leaving (*second fix*). As you can see in Chart 1, the stock was out of favor (*third fix* part I), providing a great entry point.

Disney: Chart 1 (*Third Fix Part I—Out of Favor*)

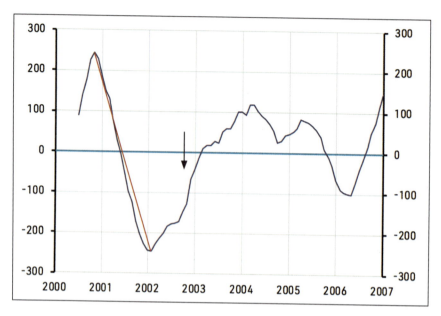

Momentum chart showing rate of change relative to the Y axis.

The second chart shows how all of a sudden, in anticipation of a management change, momentum started picking up (*third fix* part II) and the stock began its recovery.

Disney: Chart 2 (Third Fix Part II—Momentum)

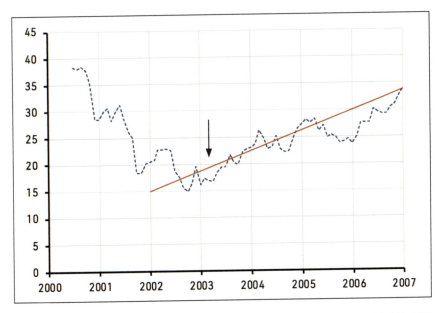

Momentum chart showing Stock Price / S&P 500.

The results can be seen in Disney's stock price, as shown in Chart 3.

Disney: Chart 3—Results

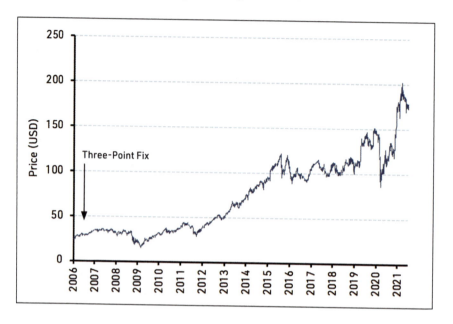

Microsoft

Microsoft was a leading technology stock in the tech boom of the late 1990s. When the bubble finally collapsed, tech stocks, which made up the NASDAQ, stayed down over the next 10 years because valuations had become so extended in the boom.

Meanwhile, Microsoft's business and earnings continued to do well over this 10-year period, while the stock price continued to drift lower, and eventually the stock reached a level where it became attractively priced on a valuation basis (*first fix*). Microsoft's growth story continued despite the terrible stock performance (*second fix*).

You can see in Chart 1 just how out of favor Microsoft was between 2010 and 2011. Wall Street started recognizing the compelling valuation and momentum began picking up (Chart 2). We now had a good entry point for the Three-Point Fix. Chart 3 shows the performance after the Three-Point Fix.

Microsoft: Chart 1 (Third Fix Part I—Out of Favor)

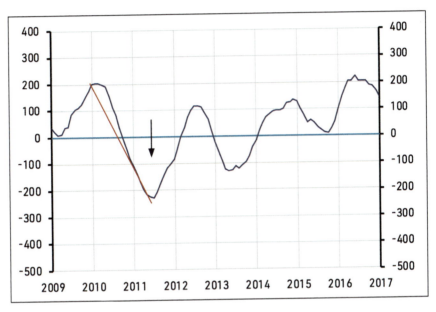

Momentum chart showing rate of change relative to the Y axis.

Microsoft: Chart 2 (Third Fix Part II—Momentum)

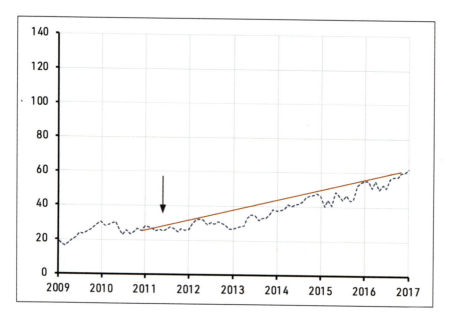

Momentum chart showing Stock Price / S&P 500.

Microsoft: Chart 3—Results

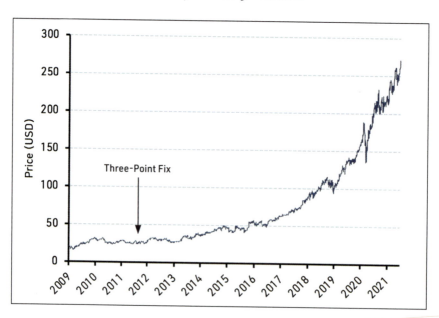

20

When to Sell

AS YOU HAVE seen, the buying discipline is very clear and straightforward. However, when to sell is much trickier. Based on my experience, here are some general rules developed over the years.

Perhaps the most important job for the investor is a constant search for stocks which are better priced and with a better story than what is already owned, thus forcing the investor to sell the most overpriced holdings and buy into the attractive new stock.

When the Stock Price Goes Higher

When a stock moves much higher and goes from being the normal 3% weight in the portfolio (based on holding around 33 stocks) to a 6% weight, and still remains attractive on a valuation basis, the strategy would be to cut the holding back to a normal 3% weight.

If the stock price runs up sharply ahead of earnings, one may continue to hold the stock until it can be replaced with something more attractive. If the stock continues to move higher, cutting the position to a half weight may make sense.

In high-dividend strategies, the P/E valuation is still a key to selling the stock, though dividend yield is also a factor. The high-dividend stocks will usually have a yield of 3% or higher before they go into the portfolio. If the dividend yield, because of a higher stock price or a dividend cut, drops below 2%, then one would look to replace the stock.

When the Stock Price Goes Lower

Unfortunately, from time to time for one reason or another, a stock in the portfolio drops more than the market, maybe −30% or more. The initial reaction is to get rid of the stock and move on, especially in taxable accounts where you can always take a tax loss. But history and experience show it doesn't pay to react indiscriminately to a sharp sell-off until doing more research.

A study of historic holdings showed that when a stock dropped more than 30%, it was sold 50% of the time and held on for the other 50%. Surprisingly, history shows that the stock should have been held in 75% of the cases, or the position added to after the drop. Another lesson the study showed was that if a company had a lot of debt, it was usually best to sell.

The example of Merck gives you an idea of how a major stock price decline was addressed.

Merck

Merck was always considered one of the top US pharmaceutical companies. The problem for value investors was that historically the P/E multiple had always been too high. But in the early 2000s, there was a huge amount of unease with the entire drug industry because so many major drugs were coming off patent. The thinking was that drug companies were not going to be able to replace a lot of their most profitable drugs. Consequently these stocks dramatically sold off.

Merck had always had a multiple of over 20x earnings, but was now down to an attractive 12x earnings with a 3.5% dividend yield.

Research led to the conclusion that Merck and the other big US drug companies, through their own research and the many joint ventures they had with a large number of biotech firms, would eventually be able to replenish their drug pipelines. Also, with the growing and aging global population overall, the long-term outlook for the industry looked very attractive. For these reasons the stock was purchased.

At the time, one of Merck's most important drugs was Vioxx, used to relieve acute arthritis pain. But the drug's alleged side effects started to attract lawsuits. Then the country's number one heart surgeon from the Mayo Clinic said publicly that he thought Vioxx represented a great risk and should be taken off the market. This drove the stock even lower. Meanwhile, the company said they would not accept a class-action settlement, but would litigate the issue on a case-by-case basis. Not good news for headline risk.

Merck was down 30% when it was originally bought, but the Vioxx issue took the stock down another 20%. Merck was now selling at

10x earnings. Vioxx continued to produce negative news, there was pressure from clients to get out of the stock. Also, a tax loss was an option that was available.

After much debate, the conclusion was Merck's chairman, Ray Gilmartin, would be replaced and his successor would come in and cut the dividend, which would take the stock down even further, creating a buying opportunity. Then we thought perhaps six months later the new chairman, wanting to look like a hero, would restore the dividend and the stock price would go back up.

With this in mind, the strategy was to sell the stock, take the tax loss, and look to buy it back when the new chairman would probably cut the dividend.

Gilmartin did get sacked, but the new chairman did not cut the dividend. And for some reason, Vioxx disappeared from the headlines. A year later, much to our chagrin, the stock was up 80%. Merck was an example of how a company with good financial fundamentals can outlast bad news.

Merck (2006–2010)

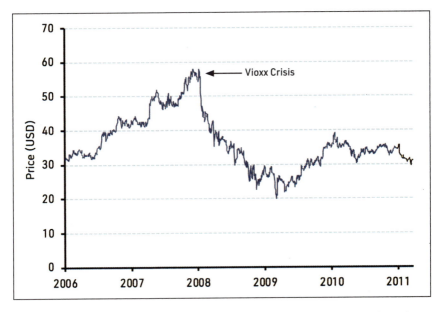

Source: Bloomberg.

Merck (2006–2021)

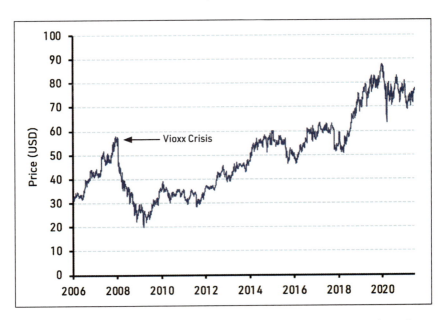

Source: Bloomberg.

SECTION FIVE

APPLYING THE STRATEGY

In Section Five, we look at how the value discipline can be applied within strategies across different sectors of the investment universe. This is important because at different times, investors want to get exposure to different kinds of stocks.

We discuss these strategies in turn:

Value

High Dividend Value

Small Cap Value

International High Dividend Value

Emerging Markets High Dividend Value

Options Writing: Covered Calls

Environmental, Social & Governance Investing

21

Value

THE FOUNDATION OF the value strategy is a low P/E discipline. This is defined as the bottom 20% of stocks in a given universe on a P/E basis. In addition, research studies show that combining low P/E with companies showing better than average earnings growth provides the best returns.

You will remember from Chapter 2, "The Value Disciplines," that one should also pay attention to the other two value disciplines: price-to-book and dividend yield. In addition, it is important to focus on the various metrics covered in Chapter 10, "Research Process."

It is recommended that a value portfolio be mostly composed of large capitalization stocks due to their stability. However, there are times when one should take advantage of international and smaller cap companies when they are cheaper on a valuation basis and have better growth prospects.

Experience shows that 30–35 stocks in a portfolio provides ample diversification. Initially each stock will have a 3% weighting to avoid concentration risk. The combination of these two portfolio construction principles provides better than average downside protection.

The goal should be to hold stocks for the long term, which has the added advantage of being very tax efficient.

The following chapters cover a series of investing strategies that all share the P/E discipline of the value strategy as the main starting point.

22

High Dividend Value

WITH THE HIGH Dividend strategy one adds a dividend component to the P/E discipline, which provides considerable additional downside protection.

While this strategy has historically performed well in up-markets, it especially has offered additional downside protection in weaker markets. As a result, the strategy has been referred to as the "safety net" of investing.

The three components of the High Dividend strategy are:

1. **P/E Multiple**—the foundation of all of the strategies.

2. **Dividend Yield**—the objective is to purchase stocks with at least a 3% yield.

3. **Dividend Growth**—This is the key to the strategy, to enable a portfolio to keep up with the market in strong up periods. Dividend growth in the 10% range is the objective.

The following graphic shows the results of a study done by Standard & Poor's, tracking the performance of the highest-yielding stocks, compared to the lowest-yielding stocks (i.e., growth stocks), and the S&P 500 Index. This study dates back to 1956 when the S&P 500 Index was first introduced and covers the period 1957–2009.

As we can see, the results are amazing. The highest-yielding stocks return almost four times as much as the index and almost 10 times as much as the lowest-yielding stocks over the period.

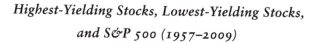

Highest-Yielding Stocks, Lowest-Yielding Stocks, and S&P 500 (1957–2009)

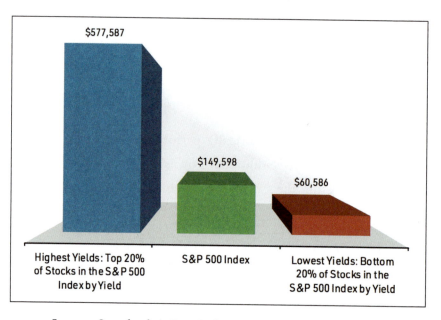

Source: Standard & Poor's Company. Cumulative Returns 1957 through 2009. Assumes annual rebalancing and reinvested dividends. Highest is top 20% / Lowest is bottom 20%.

Dividends in Recessions

In Chapter 4, we saw how S&P 500 dividends, beginning in 1940, grew consistently even though the market went through 12 recessions over the next 80 years. The only exception was the 2009–2010 recession when banks were forced by the government's TARP program to cut or eliminate their dividends. Since then, S&P 500 dividends are back to all-time highs. What we saw in Chapter 4 is that even through recessions and when stock prices have gone down, companies have found a way to maintain their dividends, thus providing investors with considerable downside protection.

As an example of how dividends have held up in recessions, we reproduce one of the Chapter 4 charts below.

S&P 500 Index and Dividends/Share (1972–1976)

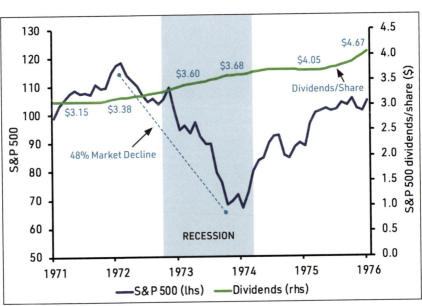

Source: Bloomberg, 2021.

The Dead Decade

A more recent experience demonstrates how dividends provide strong downside protection. This was the Dead Decade of 2000–2010, which started with the collapse of the technology stocks in 2000, followed by the horror of 9/11 in 2001, and then by the disastrous Financial Crisis that hit the market in 2008. All in all, the decade was one of the worst periods in market history.

At the beginning of the decade in 2000, our High Dividend portfolio had a 3.5% dividend yield. By the end of the decade, the dividend yield, based on cost, grew to 7.75% because of dividend increases. Also, the value of the portfolio almost doubled over that time, while the overall market was actually down. This shows the power of a high-dividend strategy in difficult markets! This is illustrated in the following chart.

Dividend Income and Yield at Cost During the Dead Decade (1999–2011)

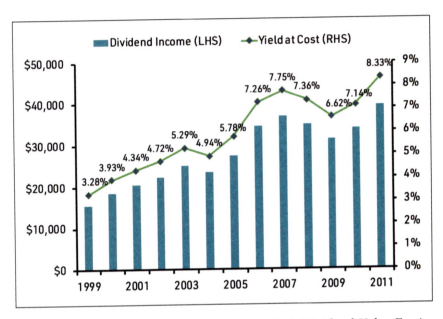

Cumulative Total Return: High Dividend Value Equity, +94.01; S&P 500, −4.48.

Kruger Fowler's Mother

Back in 1992 when I started the High Dividend strategy, a focus on dividend-yielding stocks was not at all popular with market participants. The strategy category at that time was called Equity Income. It focused only on dividend yield and was mostly made up of utility stocks. Ours was a completely different strategy. In addition to yield, the focus combined P/E, broader industry diversification and dividend growth.

One day a good friend and Wall Street veteran, Kruger Fowler, called to say he heard we had developed a new dividend strategy. He had an interesting story to tell about why he became a dividend believer.

For the last 30 years, Kruger had been responsible for his mother's investments. Because she wasn't satisfied with the income she was getting from a heavily weighted bond portfolio, he decided to put her in high-dividend stocks in order to get more income.

Meanwhile, over the years, he had been managing portfolios for some of the most sophisticated and wealthy clients on Wall Street. He would only look at his mother's portfolio once a year and maybe make a minor adjustment.

After his mother passed away, he was shocked to discover her portfolio was the best performing portfolio of all his clients. His conclusion was that maybe there was something to these dividends.

23

Small Cap Value

THERE ARE OFTEN periods when small cap stocks outperform everything else. The problem for portfolio managers is the small cap market is volatile, often making it difficult for investors to stay with the strategy. The low P/E discipline helps reduce this downside risk.

The Small Cap Value strategy uses the same research process as the value strategy, with the only difference being size. In small cap portfolios the focus is on stocks that generally have a market cap of $3 billion or less at purchase.

The following study shows that the smallest 20% of stocks by market cap in the S&P 500 outperformed the overall S&P 500 over the period from 1968–2020. The compound annualized return for the S&P 500 index was 10.1% over this period, but for the smallest 20% of stocks it was 14.6%.

A further observation on the study is that small caps tend to go down more than the market in sharp down periods but then do much better in recovery years (see the circled examples in the table).

Value & Small Cap Stocks Outperform

Years	S&P 500	Bottom 20% by Size	Years	S&P 500	Bottom 20% by Size
1968	11.0	74.2	1996	23.0	20.6
1969	−8.4	−27.9	1997	33.4	26.6
1970	3.9	3.3	1998	28.6	2.1
1971	14.3	14.3	1999	21.0	16.4
1972	18.9	5.9	2000	−9.1	8.6
1973	−14.7	−23.6	2001	−11.9	20.3
1974	−26.5	−11.5	2002	−22.1	−16.0
1975	(37.2)	(62.8)	2003	(28.7)	(67.9)
1976	23.9	52.8	2004	10.9	19.2
1977	−7.2	9.0	2005	4.9	3.5
1978	6.6	14.5	2006	15.8	19.2
1979	18.6	42.4	2007	5.5	−7.2
1980	32.4	30.6	2008	−37.0	−41.3
1981	−4.9	17.4	2009	(26.5)	(85.5)
1982	21.5	41.9	2010	15.1	24.1
1983	22.6	48.2	2011	2.1	−1.0
1984	6.3	1.2	2012	16.0	19.7
1985	31.7	19.8	2013	32.4	42.1
1986	18.7	11.4	2014	13.7	12.2
1987	5.3	7.1	2015	1.4	2.5
1988	12.5	22.6	2016	12.0	19.2
1989	31.7	20.5	2017	21.8	15.1
1990	−3.1	−22.3	2018	−4.4	−6.4
1991	30.5	40.9	2019	31.5	20.7
1992	7.6	21.5	2020	18.3	0.23
1993	10.1	15.7	Compound Annualized Returns		
1994	1.3	2.9	1968–2020	10.1%	14.6%
1995	37.6	25.2			

Source: S&P Corp, FactSet Research, SCCM 2021.

160

Small Cap Value vs. Small Cap Growth

A major misconception among investors is that any investment in small cap stocks should be made in small cap growth stocks. The record says otherwise.

A Morningstar study done back in 2005, presented below, shows that over a 78-year period, a dollar invested in small cap value grew to over $20,000, while a dollar in small cap growth lagged way behind at $1,700. Even so, it is estimated the majority of the money that has historically been invested in small caps has gone into small cap growth.

Growth of $1 Invested in 1927

Years	1927	2005
Small Cap Growth	$1	$1,723
Small Cap Value	$1	$20,920

Sources: Ibbotson Associates and Morningstar Inc. 2007.

The above study has not been updated but the big reason small cap value has done so well over the long term is because takeovers are a big part of small cap performance. And most takeover activity occurs in the small cap value universe as opposed to the growth space. Most companies are continually trying to grow their business and have two options: grow it organically or by acquisition.

For instance, there is constant consolidation going on in the banking area where the mid-size banks are buying the smaller cap banks in order to stay competitive. Also, in advertising, one of the largest firms made a statement in 2020 that they made 60 new purchases globally of small advertising agencies in order to broaden their international penetration. Most of those acquisitions were too small to show up in the financial press.

24

———

International High
Dividend Value

T HERE ARE TIMES when international low P/E stocks are dramatically cheaper than their US equivalents. While some international stocks and markets can be more volatile than the US, stock market history shows that having a dividend discipline goes a long way to reduce that risk.

In constructing international portfolios, because of volatility, approximately 40–50 stocks are used for diversification and risk management purposes, with no more than 15% in any one industry and no more than 5% in any one stock at cost. In addition, no more than 20% is allocated to any one country.

In looking for ideas in the international area, there are extensive databases that one can use to screen for ideas. These screens can be run by country, industry, or a combination thereof. Thereafter we use the metrics outlined in the High Dividend chapter.

The following pie chart shows how large the international market is compared to our US market.

Share of World GDP in US and Rest of the World

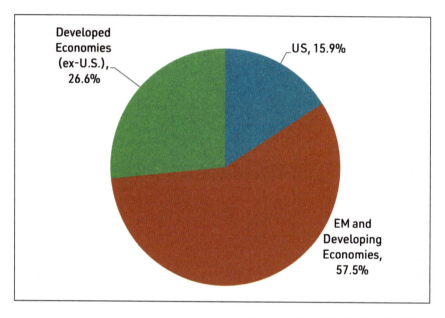

Source: *The World Bank, 2021.*

Because of the huge size of the international market, the universe of companies paying dividends is plainly much larger than that of the US.

International Dividend Universe

The following chart shows how the universe of companies paying dividends is much larger in international markets than in the US. The chart shows the number of companies with a market cap over $1 billion and a dividend yield over 3%. This tells us that there is a good pool of companies here from which to seek possible investments.

Companies with Market Cap Over $1 Billion
and Dividend Yield Over 3%

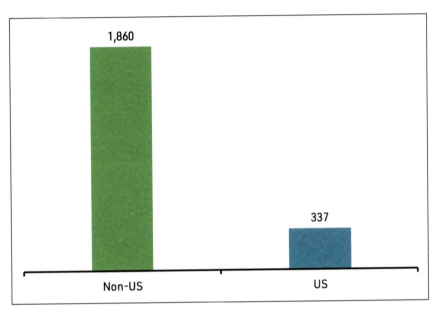

Source: SCCM Research 2021.

Dividend Advantage

The following study shows how international stocks with high and growing dividend yields have dramatically outperformed international stocks with low dividend yields and no dividend growth.

International Relative Performance of Dividend Yield Combined with Dividend Growth

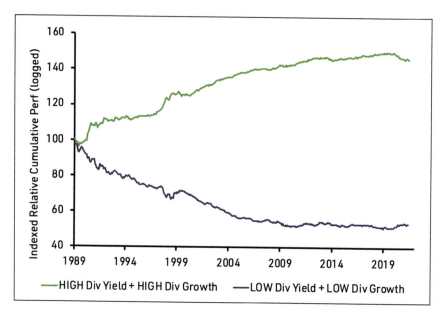

Source: Merrill Lynch.

In summary, there are times when international stocks are a lot cheaper than their US counterparts. Accordingly, some exposure to international stocks can make good investment sense, especially given the strong historical performance data for international high-dividend stocks that have growing dividends.

25

Emerging Markets High
Dividend Value

A PORTION OF THE international investment universe is categorized as emerging markets (EM), such as China, Russia, India, Brazil, Indonesia, etc. Because of these markets' enormous potential, it makes sense to consider a separate allocation as part of an international investment portfolio. These stocks tend to be even more volatile than the international developed market stocks, so the dividend discipline is even more important in this strategy for downside protection.

Emerging markets represent some of the fastest growing markets in the world. The following chart shows how emerging market GDP has been growing dramatically as a proportion of the world total.

Contribution to World GDP Growth (PPP) (1980–2024F)

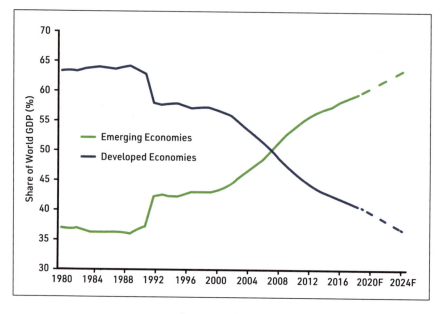

Source: NatixisPRCG. FactSet. IMF WEO.
PPP represents Purchasing Power Parity.

Emerging Markets Growth

The growth in emerging market consumers is explosive, not only compared to the US, but also compared to other developed markets. There is a continuing sharp increase in the number of EM households with an income level high enough to provide some disposable income.

The proliferation of cell phones in emerging markets is an indication of how much their economies have grown and how much room they still have for further growth as e-commerce booms in these markets.

The following chart highlights the growth of the middle class. The projections for the next decade are phenomenal, with far-reaching ramifications.

The Middle Class as a Proportion of Total Population

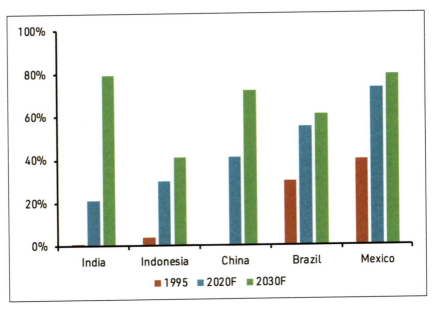

Source: SCCM Research.

Dividends: Addressing Risk

While the growth potential of emerging markets is extraordinary, volatility is also much higher than we find in developed markets.

Emerging market stocks with high dividend yields and dividend growth dramatically outperform those with low dividend yields and low dividend growth. This is very similar to what we saw in the case of international developed high-dividend stocks.

Summary

As discussed, emerging market stocks are volatile. The dividend discipline helps address this. These markets continue to have compelling growth prospects and an investment allocation is certainly worth considering.

26

Options Writing:
Covered Calls

THE SHARP DROP in bond yields following a 30-year bond bull market has caused investors to look for higher-yielding investments. A covered call writing strategy can be a good alternative.

The concept is to write options on 25–40% of the High Dividend portfolio, resulting in a total yield between 7–8%. Historically half the return has consistently come from the dividend yield of the underlying portfolio and the other half from call option premiums.

Besides higher current income, the strategy provides additional downside protection. A key to the strategy is the potential equity upside from being long 60–75% of the underlying stocks in the portfolio (i.e., the portion not covered by options).

Performance vs. Bonds

An example of how this strategy can perform relative to bonds can be seen in the following 10-year performance data. The strategy has outperformed the five-year bond by a factor of nine, the 10-year bond by a factor of nearly six, and almost doubled the return of junk bonds.

Performance of Options Writing Strategy Since Inception,
Bond Comparison (12/31/2010–12/31/2020)

Options Writing Strategy	**+115.5%**
5-Year Bond	+19.5%
10-Year Bond	+18.3%
Junk Bond	+68.4%

Alternative to Bonds

The performance of the strategy relative to bonds has been dramatic, but an objection to the strategy is that, unlike bonds, there is no maturity date. Holding the 10-year bond means you are guaranteed to get your money back at maturity. This might sound appealing on the surface, but with yields so low, the loss of principal could be considerable if the bond holder has to sell before 10 years.

While equities have no maturity date, if you look at the 10-year performance history of the lowest P/E stocks, you will see that in every period, the results are dramatically better than the return from a bond yielding 2%. These results are shown in the following table.

S&P 500 Bottom 20% by P/E—Annualized 10-Year Returns

	Bottom 20% by P/E
2011–2020	10.70%
2010–2019	13.25%
2009–2018	15.42%
2008–2017	11.45%
2007–2016	9.55%
2006–2015	9.58%
2005–2014	11.06%
2004–2013	12.05%
2003–2012	11.73%
2002–2011	9.07%
2001–2010	10.57%
2000–2009	10.92%
1999–2008	7.03%
1998–2007	12.45%
1997–2006	16.13%
1996–2005	16.20%
1995–2004	18.55%
1994–2003	16.46%
1993–2002	14.49%
1992–2001	17.36%
1991–2000	20.23%
1990–1999	15.72%

Summary

Call writing is not as tax efficient as the underlying High Dividend strategy, but for tax-exempt investment accounts it is especially attractive.

27

Environmental, Social & Governance (ESG) Investing

OCIALLY RESPONSIBLE INVESTING has been around for a
long time but in the past, performance has not been competitive
because companies in the US are aggressively focused on the
bottom line, making social responsibility a secondary consideration.

However, the climate for ESG investing is changing and this theme
is more popular with investors today than it has been in the past.
The current generation is less focused solely on the bottom line
and more sensitive to ESG considerations. For this reason, the
time may be right for combining the value disciplines with social
agenda investing.

It is still early days for this strategy, and it will be interesting to review the performance data after five and 10 years.

———————

Now that we have reviewed some applications of the value discipline within a range of investing strategies, we move on to Section Six, where we discuss the nature of the market.

SECTION SIX

THE MARKET

Ben Graham, when asked why investors and professionals did not do well in the market, answered: "because of their lack of understanding of the "the beast." When asked what was meant by "the beast," he said "**the market.**"

In view of this, in Section Six we review the nature of the market and attempt to reach a better understanding—the aim being to equip investors to achieve better investment results.

The primary characteristics of the market we investigate are bear markets and recessions. In addition, we look at some other things investors periodically have to deal with—such as speculative bubbles, record debt levels, collapse of consumer confidence, and spikes in interest rates.

We begin with bear markets and recessions.

28

The History of Bear
Markets and Recessions

THIS CHAPTER IS important because bear markets and recessions are where most investment mistakes are made.

That is because investors are always trying to figure out, usually unsuccessfully, how to avoid recessions and bear markets. Investors have good company here, as economists and market strategists also spend a lot of time worrying about the next recession and what might cause it.

Because recessions and bear markets usually go hand in hand, we treat them together in this chapter and look to see where they overlap and where they don't. But first, we will define what is meant by a correction, a bear market, and a recession.

1. **Market correction:** This is a 10% drop in the market from its recent highs. Approximately four out of five corrections have been great buying opportunities. As markets tend to go higher, "buy on the dip" becomes the mantra. However, it is the other one-fifth of the time, when the correction is not a good buying opportunity, which is trouble.

2. A **bear market** occurs when a correction extends and results in a 20% drop in the market. Bear markets tend to sneak up on investors because of the "buy on the dip" mentality we just mentioned.

3. A **recession** has historically been defined as two down quarters in succession of gross domestic product (GDP), as decided by a US government committee. The problem is, by the time the government officially declares a recession, it is usually well underway. Also, since recessions usually come after a bear market, they don't give any advance warning of the bear market.

Before we address each of the recessions and bear markets over the last 70 years, let's make a few general observations:

- The biggest trap for investors is the fact that "buy on the dip" becomes a mantra in an up-market and usually there is no warning when it slips below a 20% correction and into a bear market.

- Once the bear market is officially established, history shows that at this point half of the correction is usually over.

- What we see is that when a bear market is over, markets tend to explode off their lows. Looking at historic charts, it appears it would be easy to buy at these points. This is the beauty of hindsight! But a closer inspection shows this bottoming period can last for as long as a year. Also, there are usually a lot of false rallies from the bottom, making it much more difficult to detect the final low than it would appear from looking back at historic charts.

- The explosion off the bear market lows is dramatic and tends to wipe out the entire bear market loss over the next 12 months. We will point out at the end of this chapter how history shows that if one were to miss out on the one-year recovery from the bottom of these bear markets, it would negate the entire advantage of being in equities.

Next, we review the relationship between recessions and bear markets over the last 70 years. We start with the recession of 1969–1970.

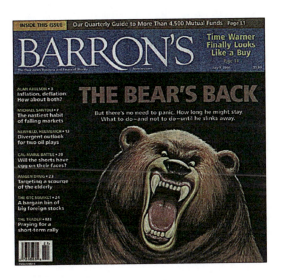

Copyright 2008 Dow Jones & Company Inc. All rights reserved.

1969–1970

At the time, this was the worst bear market since the Great Depression. The accompanying chart shows the market peaked in October of 1968, marking the end of a long bull market. For many years prior to that peak, all 10% market corrections were good buying opportunities. Therefore, when the market finally peaked, it had already experienced many "buy on the dip" opportunities.

Before the bear market became official, there was a period of a year where the market rallied and failed multiple times, as it took a long time for investors to believe the end of a long bull market had actually occurred.

You can also see a typical explosion off the bottom. In two years, the rally wiped out the entire bear market drop. While the bottom looks like a v-shaped recovery in the chart, it actually took six months to form a bottom.

1969–1970 Recession (S&P 500)

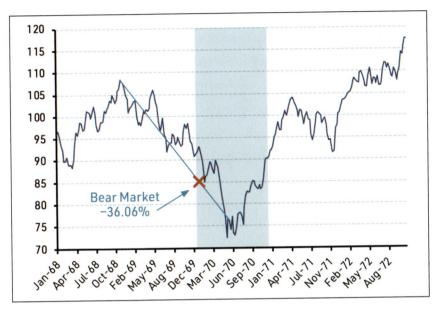

X: *Bear market (–20%) was official 1/29/1970.*
Shaded area shows recession.

Source: SCCM.

1973–1974

The steep rise following the market's 1970 lows was dominated by institutions buying what they felt were the highest-quality companies, the so-called Nifty Fifty. As we remarked earlier in the book, buyers thought the stocks of these companies were worthy of any price because their future prospects were so phenomenal. The result was the "buy on the dip" strategy had again become deeply ingrained among investors.

After the market peaked in January of 1973, there was a correction of 10% into June 1973. This looked like another buying opportunity, because the market recovered sharply into the beginning of 1974. But the next correction established the bear market and institutions gradually started heading for the exits. By the middle of 1974, a full-fledged panic was underway and the Nifty Fifty bubble was history.

Again, the explosion off the lows was dramatic, but it took five months for the bottom to form.

1973–1974 Recession (S&P 500)

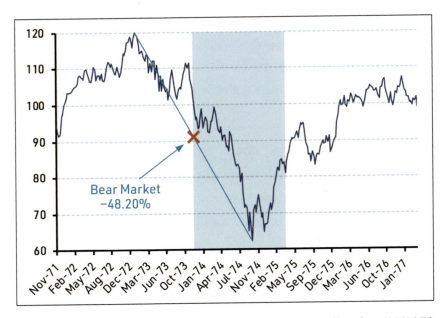

X: Bear market 20% was official 11/27/1973.
Shaded area shows recession.

Source: SCCM.

1981–1983

The market took some time to regain confidence after the severe downturn of 1974–1975. Company earnings recovered, but enthusiasm for stocks came back only slowly.

With little interest in the stock market, alternatives to stocks became popular; among them, real estate, art, and gold, which seemed to serve as a hedge against a dramatic run-up in inflation. So even while valuations in the stock market were reasonable, Fed Chairman Paul Volcker pushed interest rates up to the stratospheric level of 20%, resulting in a double dip recession.

The market sold-off as a reaction to the rate hike, while the banking industry got squeezed by loans made to companies leveraged to real estate. Continental Illinois, the seventh largest bank in the country, went bankrupt. But because valuations were at one of the cheapest levels in history, the market had a dramatic recovery despite sky-high interest rates.

1981–1983 Recession (S&P 500)

X: *Bear market –20% was official 5/29/1982.*
Shaded area shows recessions.

Source: SCCM.

1987

Because valuations in the early 1980s were so attractive, investors gradually started to come back into the market after the 1982 lows. As confidence built, speculation picked up dramatically, and for the first time we heard the expression "melt-up market"—describing markets that went up without at least a 10% correction.

Even so, institutions remembered the collapse of the Nifty Fifty and started to worry about the market's speculative fever. So they were talked into buying something called "portfolio insurance"— computer algorithms that would, they thought, protect them in a down market.

Portfolio insurance didn't work. Stocks suffered a 25% drop in one day and blew through all the puts on the market, making them worthless. This was Black Monday, the biggest one-day percentage drop in history. But no recession followed and the recovery from the drop was v-shaped.

1987 *Bear Market (S&P 500)*

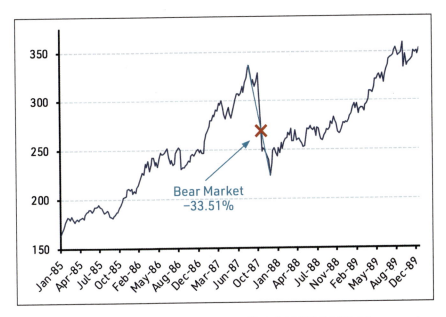

X: *Bear market –20% was official 10/17/1987. No recession.*

Source: SCCM.

191

1990–1991

Because we had a serious one-day collapse in 1987, a lot of speculation was taken out of the market. So when the economy slowed and produced a recession in 1990, there was no bear market.

The 1990–1991 recession was a reaction to the huge build-up in the real estate market that developed after the bear market of the early 1970s. Investors decided to buy real estate rather than equities. The overpriced real estate market, bid up by speculators, led to the major banking crisis we talked about in the review of 100 years of market history in Chapter 1. We noted more banks went bankrupt during that recession than in the Great Depression of the 1930s.

With speculators out of equities, the recession did not produce a bear market, although we came close. The market dropped 19% in late 1990 and had a huge recovery from the lows.

1990–1991 Recession (S&P 500)

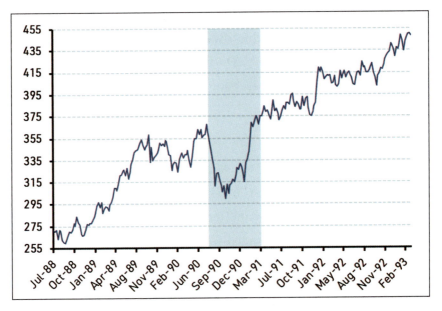

No bear market. Shaded area shows recession.

Source: SCCM.

2001

The 10-year run-up from the lows of 1990 was the strongest 10-year period in market history. During the decade, investors became completely fascinated with technology and "buy on the dip" again became a Wall Street mantra.

The market peaked in April of 2000 and by April of 2001 we were officially in a bear market. That same month, a recession also began. The recovery from the bear market and the recession was then interrupted by the shock of the terrorist attacks on September 11, 2001. While the recession officially ended in November of 2001, the market received a shock when the Twin Towers were struck, resulting in an unusual resumption of the bear market and a second leg down.

The back-to-back bear markets took the wind out of the Tech Bubble. NASDAQ, the index for technology companies, dropped 80% over the next 10 years.

2001 Recession (S&P 500)

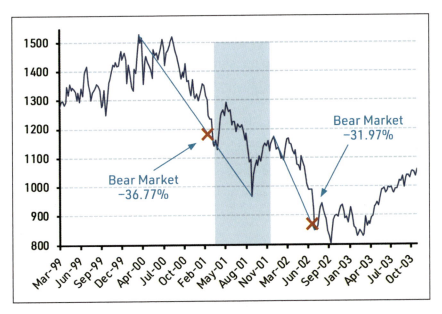

X: *Bear market –20% was official 2/12/2001.*
X: *Bear market –20% was official 7/10/2002.*
Shaded area shows recession.

Source: SCCM.

2008–2009

If things weren't bad enough between 2000 and 2003, the Financial Crisis, which started in 2007, resulted in the most severe bear market since 1929. The market dropped 65%.

After the market peaked in June of 2007, the highs were tested in September of 2007, after which there was a period of buying on dips until 2008. As of June of 2008, the recession still had not been declared. Even so, the news for institutions got worse and the market rolled over.

Between October of 2008 and February of 2009, when it appeared that the market was finally making new lows, stocks continued to move lower because there was fear over a possible collapse of the financial system.

The fear was of a possible domino-effect panic throughout the entire economy. The market was saved when the government bailed out the banks, but the public was not happy with the way it was handled— the big guys got help, while mom and pop didn't. It was also a really hard time to pick a market bottom because the rallies kept failing.

2007–2009 Recession (S&P 500)

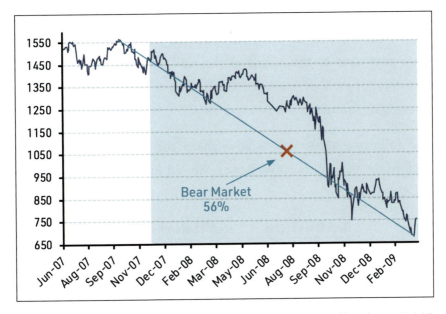

X: *Bear market −20% was official 7/15/2008.*
Shaded area shows recession.

Source: SCCM.

Post-Bear Market Bounce

Earlier we talked about investors not being in the market when there is an explosion to the upside at the end of a bear market. And if investors miss out on the big bounces, this wipes out any advantage of being in equities at all.

The following table shows how sharp the snapbacks were after each of the bear markets we have reviewed in this chapter (with the exception of 9/11).

Bear Market End	Next 12 Months (S&P 500)
6/13/1949	42.07%
10/22/1957	31.02%
6/26/1962	32.66%
10/7/1966	33.06%
5/26/1970	43.73%
10/3/1974	37.96%
8/12/1982	59.40%
12/4/1987	22.40%
9/21/2001	−12.50%
7/23/2002	17.94%
3/9/2009	68.57%

Source: SCCM.

Summary

After reading about bear markets and recessions, how they form and how they proceed, and how a sharp recovery usually follows, it might be a good idea to go back and re-read Chapter 8, "Long-Term Value." This might give you confidence in equities by knowing that if you invest on a five-year basis and stay disciplined about price, you can do well in spite of all the madness in the stock market.

29

Secular Bear Markets

FOR THE LONG-TERM investor, the good news is that the stock market tends to go up about 75% of the time and down only 25% of the time, and the bounce back from down markets tends to be very swift. But there are periods when the market is flat or negative for a long period of time, and these periods are called secular bear markets.

During my career on Wall Street, there have been two such markets. The most recent was the 2000–2010 Dead Decade, which we discussed in Chapter 22 about the High Dividend Strategy. During the 10 years, the market was down 10% due to the collapse of the Tech Bubble, 9/11 and the Financial Crisis, but the High Dividend strategy itself was up over 100% during the same time, thanks to attractive valuations, growing earnings, and dividends.

My earlier experience with a secular bear market occurred between 1968 and 1982, which we discussed in the "Market History" chapter.

The following chart, referenced earlier, covers this period, showing that while the market was flat, there were a lot of market swings between 700 and 1,000.

Dow Jones Industrial Average (1964–1982)

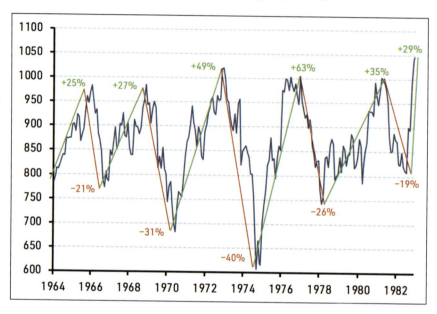

Source: Bloomberg, SCCM Research.

As we have discussed, the reason why stocks go up over time is because earnings and dividends tend to go up over time. So you might wonder what happened to earnings during these 18 years of a secular bear market.

It turns out that earnings actually tripled during the bear market, but multiples on the Dow Jones index were so inflated by the Nifty Fifty craze that the index stayed flat. **But during that same time, the bottom 20% of stocks on a P/E basis (value) were not flat, but rather up over 1,000%.**

In sum, periods of a secular bear market tend to get a lot of publicity, but the key to successful stock investing is to focus on valuations, earnings, and dividend growth, and stay the course.

30

Melt-up Markets

In the Long Term,
Value Wins

W ALL STREET DEFINES a "melt-up market" as one
in which the S&P 500 goes up for 200 days without
a correction. As we saw in Chapter 28, a correction is
defined as a market drop of more than 10%.

A melt-up period tends to start following a recession or bear
market, when most investors have gone into cash. Then, gradually,
they start coming back into equities, drawn by what they see as
attractive valuations.

As stocks climb steadily higher, investors increasingly start chasing the
trend and ignoring valuations. This eventually leads to a speculative

bubble and finally a dramatic sell-off for the market—especially for the most inflated stocks that drove the melt-up.

It is hard to believe just how many melt-up markets we have had in the last 80 years. And because such markets favor high P/E growth stocks, it is also hard to believe that value dramatically outperforms growth over the long term.

The following table lists all the major melt-up periods that have occurred in the last 80 years, in order of duration.

Periods More Than 500 Days without a 10% Correction

Date Range	Number of Days
1990–1997	1,767 days
2003–2007	1,154 days
2011–2015	913 days
1962–1966	830 days
1984–1987	780 days
1950–1953	681 days
1943–1945	639 days
1953–1955	510 days

Schafer Cullen, 2013.

Following are a few brief comments on each period.

1990–1997

This is currently the biggest melt-up period in market history. We talked earlier about how the tech stocks were presumed to usher in a new era, or a new paradigm. The enthusiasm drove multiples to nosebleed levels. The eventual correction was equally dramatic.

2003–2007

This melt-up in equities developed following the collapse of the tech stocks, followed by the World Trade Center attacks. The combination of these events got everyone out of the market. When this recovery started, there was very little selling left, enabling the market to run 1,154 days without a correction.

2011–2015

This melt-up followed the 2008–2009 Financial Crisis, when the banking industry came close to melting down and the world was worried about the unintended consequences leading to a financial panic. Again, many investors had gotten out of the market, reacting to scary headlines about the possibility of major banks collapsing. The prospect was especially alarming because the major banks held most investors' assets. After the controversial bailout of the financial and auto industries, confidence returned and the market exploded upward.

1962–1966

At the time, this was the biggest melt-up period to date. It was the result of a gradual buildup in enthusiasm for stocks which had slowly developed following the market's long, steady recovery from the 1940s.

1984–1987

This was the first time I can remember the term "melt-up" being used by the press. Stocks were extremely cheap coming out of the double-dip recession of the early 1980s, producing a market that was going up every day. Institutions, remembering the 1970s, set up Portfolio Insurance to hedge against a market decline. The insurance didn't work and that was the end of the melt-up.

1950–1953, 1943–1945, 1953–1955

All of these melt-ups were considered fairly dramatic at the time, but investors were still nervous about the 1930s experience, so excessive optimism never built up. The first sign of an economic slowdown ended each of the melt-ups.

Why Long-Term Value Wins

Why is it that value outperforms growth?

Looking at performance on a five-year basis, in the melt-up periods when value trails, it is usually only modestly. However, in all the other periods when value outperforms, the difference is fairly dramatic. To see how this plays out, refer to Chapter 5, "Value vs. Growth."

31

Bubbles

IN THE PRIOR chapter we saw how melt-up markets can lead to extreme speculation. This can gradually develop into a stock market bubble.

As we have discussed US bubbles earlier in the book, in this chapter we will only highlight the similarities of the three major US bubbles. Meanwhile, bubbles have had a long history and before we start on the US bubbles, we will take a look at two of history's highest profile examples, plus the Japanese bubble of 1990.

Tulip Mania (1634–1637)

The tulip was introduced to the Netherlands from the Ottoman Empire. Gradually, enthusiasm for tulips grew and prices started going higher. Then speculators began buying, which drove prices even higher.

Eventually, all classes of Dutch society were involved in tulip bulb speculation and many were trading all of their worldly possessions for a single tulip bulb.

Prices eventually peaked and then imploded, throwing the Netherlands into a depression that lasted for many years.

Tulipmania in 17th Century Netherlands

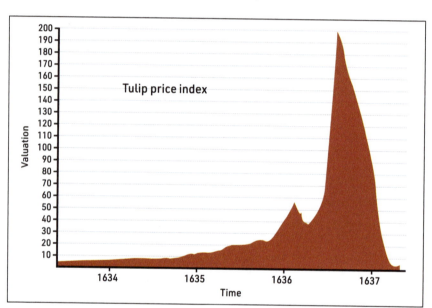

Source: Author.

The South Sea Bubble (1716–1720)

The South Sea Bubble was based on the shares of the South Sea Company, an international trading company granted special trading rights by the British government in the South Sea, which encompassed South America.

South Sea Company executives misled investors and embellished the commercial value of the company, causing the shares to soar. When the sham was exposed, the shares collapsed, which you can see in the following chart.

Interestingly, one of the victims of the bubble, who was completely wiped out, was the scientist Isaac Newton. His quote after he lost everything was: "I can calculate the movement of stars, but not the madness of men."

South Sea Company (1719–1722)

Source: Wikipedia.

Japanese Bubble

In the 1980s the Japanese economy was the strongest in the world and its technology companies like Sony and Canon dominated world trade.

Japan's success in the late 1980s was evident in new high-end Japanese restaurants popping up in cities around the world and top hotels crowded with Japanese businessmen. Japanese investors were also big buyers of US real estate—two high-profile examples were Rockefeller Center and Pebble Beach golf course.

After P/E multiples for the Nikkei Index peaked out at 100x earnings, the decline started and as the following chart shows, despite having some impressive rallies over the next 10 years, the index was still down 65% from its 1990 highs.

Nikkei 225 Index (1988–2006)

Loss of 80% in the Nikkei 225 from its peak

Source: Yahoo Finance data.

208

US Bubbles

We have already touched on the three major US bubbles: the Roaring 20s aftermath, the Nifty Fifty experience, and the Tech Bubble.

All these bubbles were similar in that first there was a period of little to no interest in the market for one reason or another. Then, gradually, money started flowing into the market, driving prices and valuations higher, resulting in a melt-up market environment. Then came the bubble from overvaluation, followed by a collapse.

Each period was considered a new era for investing and in fact it was, but as great as all the companies were that benefited from the build-up, they became victims of having their stock price get way ahead of earnings.

Another common trait of all three of these bubbles was that earnings for all the bubble companies continued to grow, despite the long decline in their stock prices. As you can see in the following table, it took the market a long time to reach a point where the stock price could be justified on a valuation basis. In each of the examples given here, 10 years after the peak the companies' stock prices had posted a negative return. Interestingly, in every case, these stocks eventually became attractive for value investors.

Major Expansion	Top Stock	P/E Multiple at Peak	Return 5 Years Later	Return 10 Years Later
Roaring 20s				
	Radio Corp of America	73.0x	−99%	−83%
Nifty Fifty				
	Avon Products	63.0x	−58%	−66%
	Xerox	254.1x	−70%	−83%
	Polaroid	26.9x	−79%	−87%
	Eastman Kodak	24x	−66%	−42%
Tech Bubble				
	Cisco	230.4x	−78%	−67%
	Intel	50.8x	−66%	−76%
	Microsoft	79.9x	−55%	−48%
	Oracle	60.0x	−71%	−41%

Source: Bloomberg, December 2017.

32

No More
Recessions?

A BIG QUESTION AMONG investors these days is how long can the economy go without a recession, barring an extraordinary event like Covid-19?

When governments in the US and around the world are doing everything they can to keep their economies going, some investors have concluded that a recession, domestic or global, can be forestalled indefinitely.

There is a new economic theory being presented by some liberal economists called MMT (Modern Monetary Theory). The idea is that every problem can be solved by printing money. How this all plays out in the stock market will be interesting to see. But perhaps more important for investors is the example of Australia, where their stock market tracked its own course, ignoring the economy.

Over the last 75 years, there have been 12 recessions in the US, with the longest period between downturns being approximately eight years. Therefore, it is shocking to superficially observe that Australia has gone 25 years without a recession. While this seems remarkable, it can be explained by the phenomenal growth in China and Chinese demand for Australian commodities.

Meanwhile, while Australian GDP has gone up for 25 years, the Australian stock market was a very different story. On the next page we superimpose a graph of the stock market over the economy.

What you see is Australia had multiple market corrections, most of them worse than those in the United States over the same time period. Five were down more than 20%, with one down more than 50%. The takeaway here is that markets make adjustments to valuations regardless of whether there's a recession or not.

MMT or any other new policy that is cooked up shouldn't change that.

Australia—Recessions and Bear Markets

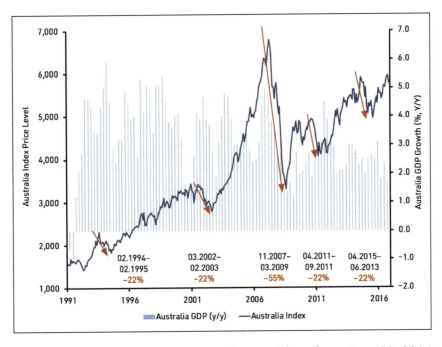

Source: Bloomberg, June 30, 2016.

Conclusion

The lesson from the Australian example is one should not use the economy to try to time the market.

33

Debt

Government—Corporate—Individual

ECONOMISTS HAVE ALWAYS tracked debt for three major categories—government, corporate, and individual. While the level of debt is always followed by Wall Street, it is not usually a major stock market factor. However, when it does become a factor, the most leveraged players tend to get wiped out.

Debt: The First 5,000 Years is a 500-page book on the subject. The book concludes that excessive debt periodically catches up with those who abuse it, with devastating consequences. There are examples of this in the case of governments, corporations, and individuals.

From time to time, Wall Street strategists frighten investors with talk about the risks of too much debt. This often gets media attention, but debt is usually not an issue for high-quality value stocks.

Below, we look at the three major categories of debt.

1. Government Debt

In our recent history, the market has periodically had to deal with the raising of the debt ceiling. With government debt at historically high levels, the ceiling can get a lot of play, especially when it becomes hotly political.

As you can see in the following chart, federal debt as a percentage of GDP has had a sharp rise since 2008. Historically, having federal debt over 100% of GDP has been a warning sign for a country and the US has reached that level.

Federal Debt as a % of GDP

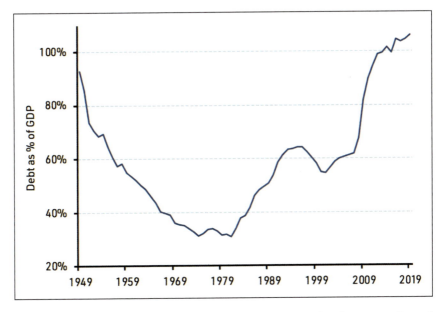

Source: Federal Reserve Board.

However, looking at government debt on a longer-term basis, the last time debt was as high as it is now relative to GDP was in 1945. If you bought stocks then, it was one of the best buying opportunities in the last 100 years. Therefore, it doesn't pay to overreact to the build-up of debt by itself. More important is whether a country has the ability to grow its way out of these high levels of debt, as happened after 1945.

While the US has always been able to manage its debt, many weaker countries have defaulted. They still managed to survive, but not on terms good for investors. An example is Argentina, which has defaulted seven times in the last 30 years.

2. Corporate Debt

The following chart covering the last three decades shows how corporate debt builds up until default rates reach unacceptable levels.

The green line on the chart shows the default rate for the more speculative high-yield bonds, once called "junk bonds." We can see that default rates are currently low, even though there has been an expansion of debt as a percentage of GDP (the blue line). This is worth keeping an eye on, especially because higher default rates tend to follow periods of debt expansion—as you can see in the chart, with the green and yellow lines usually mirroring each other.

An example of corporations getting caught with excessive debt was the conglomerates of the 1960s, which we talked about earlier in the book.

Recent Default Rate and its Projected Trend Defy Record
Ratio of Corporate Debt to US GDP

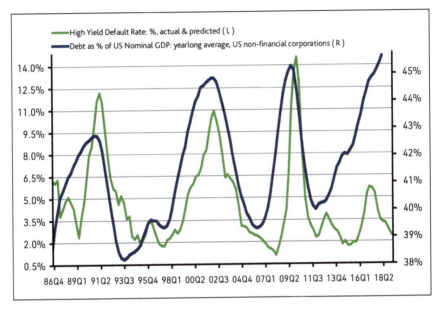

Source: Moody's Analytics.

3. Individual Debt

Individual debt statistics are important because the US economy is 75% consumer-led.

Since the 2009 Financial Crisis, student loan debt has been the fastest growing type of individual debt, followed by mortgage debt and auto loans. Meanwhile, home equity lines of credit and credit card debt have been growing at slower rates.

The following chart shows US domestic debt relative to GDP. We see that since the 2009 Financial Crisis, debt as a percentage of GDP has actually improved slightly.

The chart also shows that when consumer debt is above 131, overall growth of the economy tends to be slower, as against below 101, which has historically been a level for better growth. As the table accompanying the chart shows, GDP growth is almost twice as strong when the debt/GDP ratio is below 101 (+7.73 v. +3.98).

Private Domestic Non-Financial Debt as a Percentage of GDP

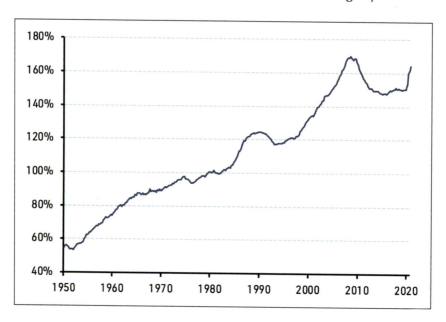

Ned Davis Research, 2018.

Nominal GDP Gain Per Annum

Debt/GBP	% Gain/Annum	% of Time
Above 131%	3.93	27.51
Between 101% and 131%	5.96	23.79
Below 101%	7.73	48.70

Excessive individual debt can have a drag on corporate earnings and the market, especially if consumer confidence declines. Again, in a corrective phase of the market, households who have leveraged up are the most impacted.

An example of excessive individual debt becoming a problem was the abuse of borrowing on margin in the 1970s (see Chapter 1, "Market History"). When the market broke, all the margin accounts were wiped out.

34

The Wall Street Quilt

THE FOLLOWING TABLE might look to you like your grandmother's quilt. But what it does is track the annual performance of all the important financial asset classes: US growth; US value; bonds; small cap; international markets; and emerging markets.

The Quilt shows that asset classes swing from best to worse, and then back again, in highly irregular fashion. This phenomenon shows you why the stock market is so unpredictable on a year-to-year basis.

As you can see in the Quilt, for example, international and emerging markets were the best performers between 2003 and 2009; and then became the worst performers between 2013 and 2018.

1997	1998	1999	2000	2001	2002	2003	2004	2005	2006	2007	2008
US Growth +36.52%	US Growth +42.16%	EM +66.84%	Bonds +11.63%	Bonds +8.43%	Bonds +10.26%	EM +55.82%	EM +25.55%	EM +34.00%	EM +32.17%	EM +39.38%	Bonds +5.24%
US Value +29.98%	International +20.00%	US Growth +28.24%	US Value +6.08%	Small Cap +2.49%	EM −6.16%	Small Cap +47.25%	International +20.25%	International +13.54%	International +26.34%	International +11.17%	Small Cap −33.79%
Small Cap +22.36%	US Value +14.68%	International +26.96%	Small Cap −3.02%	EM −2.61%	International −15.94%	International +38.59%	Small Cap +18.33%	US Value +5.82%	US Value +20.81%	US Growth +9.13%	Growth −34.92%
Bonds +9.64%	Bonds +8.67"	Small Cap +21.26%	International −14.17%	US Value −11.71%	Small Cap −20.48%	US Value +31.79%	US Value +15.71%	Small Cap +4.55%	Small Cap +18.37%	Bonds +6.97%	US Value −39.22%
International +1.78%	Small Cap −2.55%	US Value +12.73%	US Growth −22.08%	US Growth −12.73%	US Value −20.85%	US Growth +25.66%	US Growth +6.13%	US Growth +4.00%	US Growth +11.01%	US Value +1.99%	International −43.38%
EM −11.59%	EM −25.34%	Bonds −0.83%	EM −30.71%	International −21.44%	US Growth −23.59%	Bonds +4.10%	Bonds +4.34%	Bonds +2.43%	Bonds +4.33%	Small Cap −1.57%	EM −53.33%

2009	2010	2011	2012	2013	2014	2015	2016	2017	2018	2019	2020
EM +78.51%	Small Cap +26.85%	Bonds +7.84%	EM +18.23%	Small Cap +38.82%	US Growth +14.89%	US Growth +5.52%	Small Cap +21.31%	EM +37.28%	Bonds +0.01%	US Value +31.92%	US Growth +33.35%
International +31.78%	EM +18.88%	US Growth +4.65%	US Value +17.68%	US Growth +32.75%	US Value +12.36%	Bonds +0.55%	US Value +17.40%	US Growth +27.44%	US Growth −0.01%	US Growth +31.13%	Small Cap +19.93%
US Growth +31.57%	US Value +15.10%	US Value −0.48%	International +17.32%	US Value +31.99%	Bonds +5.97%	International −0.81%	EM +11.19%	International +25.03%	US Value −8.97%	Small Cap +25.49%	EM +18.25%
Small Cap +27.17%	US Growth +15.05%	Sm... Cap −4.18%	Small +16.35	International ..78%	Small Cap +4.89%	US Value −3.13%	US Growth +6.89%	US Value +15.36%	Small Cap −11.03%	International +22.01%	International +7.79%
US Value +21.17%	International +7.75%	International −12.14%	US Growth +14.61%	Bonds −2.02%	EM −2.19%	Small Cap −4.41%	Bonds +2.65%	Small Cap +14.65%	International −13.79%	EM +18.42%	Bonds +7.49%
Bonds +5.93%	Bonds +6.54%	EM −18.42%	Bonds +4.21%	EM −2.60%	International −4.90%	EM −14.92%	International +1.00%	Bonds +3.54%	EM −14.57%	Bonds +8.72%	US Value +1.34%

Source: Bloomberg, SCCM.

The chart illustrates the volatility of sector performance. Note that while value has had solid overall performance, it was rarely the best or the worst in any one year. This meant value never benefitted from all the favorable publicity and excitement from the brokerage community and financial press that was attached to other hot areas. Value just proceeded steadily.

35

Consumer
Confidence

THE CONSUMER CONFIDENCE index has been tracked by the Conference Board going back to the 1960s. Since the US economy is 75% consumer-led, this index is worth observing.

When the economy is doing well, consumer confidence will be very positive and tends to stay that way for a long period of time, and is not a market factor. However, when consumer confidence drops below 60%, history shows that level usually coincides with major market lows.

The following chart traces the consumer confidence index from 1965–2020. You can see how dips in consumer confidence coincide with recessions and stock market lows.

US Conference Board Consumer Confidence Index
(rebased to 100 in 1985)

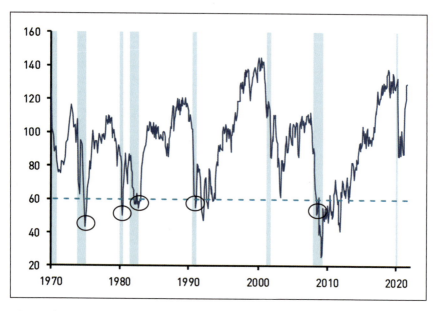

The following table shows market performance 12 months after confidence has dropped below the 60% level.

When confidence has dropped to those low levels, the economic news is usually extremely negative, with articles about retailers going bankrupt and shoppers retrenching.

Despite the negative headline news, this has proven to be a time *not* to bail out. As the table shows, one year later the S&P 500 is normally much higher. Thus, dips in consumer confidence are usually a major buying opportunity.

Consumer Confidence Under 60%	S&P 500 One Year Later
Nov 1974	+45%
May 1980	+35%
May 1982	+45%
Oct 1990	+30%
Nov 2008	+35%

36

Spikes in
Interest Rates

AFTER BEN GRAHAM laid out his two principles for successful investing—be disciplined about price and invest for the long term—he said if you followed this strategy, you could ignore everything else.

Initially, this may be met with disbelief: how can you ignore big interest rate moves like the experience of the 1970s, when interest rates spiked from 4% to 16%?

It turns out Graham was right. If you stuck with the value discipline, either low P/E or high dividend, you would have done well, as summarized in the following chart.

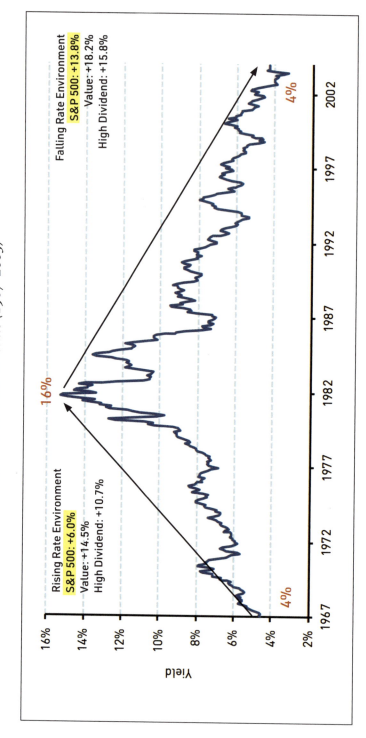

Performance of S&P 500, Value, High Dividend, and Growth During Rising and Falling Interest Rate Environments (1967–2003)

Rising Rate Environment
S&P 500: +6.0%
Value: +14.5%
High Dividend: +10.7%

Falling Rate Environment
S&P 500: +13.8%
Value: +18.2%
High Dividend: +15.8%

Value = bottom 20% of S&P 500 by P/E. High Dividend = top 20% of S&P 500 by yield.

Interest Rate Study

Over the 36-year period (1967–2003), rates went from 4% to 16%, and then back again to 4%. What jumps out from the study is that, in a rising rate environment, the low P/E value stocks (+14.5%) and the high-dividend stocks (+10.7%) dramatically outperformed the S&P 500 (+6.0%).

Not surprisingly, in the falling rate environment the overall market did dramatically better than when rates were rising (+13.8% vs. +6.0%). The value disciplines performed as well in the falling rate environment, but the relative performance was nothing like it was in the rising rate environment.

1971–1991 Study

In the following table we analyze the rolling five-year periods of the most dramatic portion of the previous graph: the 20-year period from 1971–1991. The results are similar to those of the longer-term study.

The data for the top 20% of stocks by yield and bottom 20% of stocks by P/E for five-year periods within the timeframe of this study are summarized in the table. One will note that in every five-year period, value performed well.

Performance of Top 20% by Yield and Bottom 20% by P/E in Five-Year Periods During Rising and Falling Interest Rate Environments (1971–1991)

5-Year Periods	Top 20% by Yield	Bottom 20% by P/E	5-Year Periods	Top 20% by Yield	Bottom 20% by P/E
1971–1975	6.67%	7.59%	1981–1985	25.12%	24.79%
1972–1976	12.12%	14.06%	1982–1986	25.28%	27.74%
1973–1977	10.83%	14.18%	1983–1987	18.36%	20.06%
1974–1978	14.90%	21.06%	1984–1988	15.97%	20.04%
1975–1979	24.64%	30.73%	1985–1989	18.65%	21.16%
1976–1980	16.55%	26.06%	1986–1990	7.95%	10.52%
1977–1981	12.24%	20.38%	1987–1991	12.14%	13.05%
Average 5yr Return	13.99%	19.15%	Average 5yr Return	17.64%	19.62%
S&P Avg. 5Yr Return	7.02%		S&P Avg. 5Yr Return	16.50%	

Why Did Value Do Well When Rates Spiked Higher?

The next chart shows how the inflation rate tracks almost exactly the same pattern as the previous interest rates chart. This makes obvious sense because they both tend to rise during periods of economic growth.

US CPI Y/Y % (1953–2003)

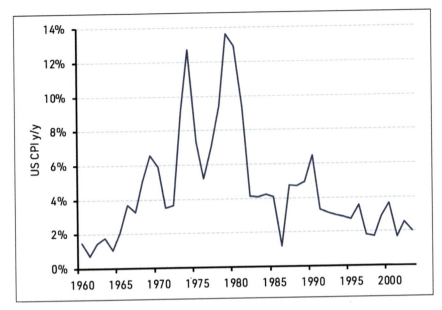

Source: Strategas.

It seems counterintuitive that low P/E stocks and high-dividend stocks should do well when interest rates are going higher. Why this is the case can be found in the following chart, which tracks the P/E multiple of the market.

We see that as rates go higher, P/E multiples contract and as rates go lower, P/E multiples expand. The result is that the value disciplines do better when P/E multiples in general are contracting. Therefore, as you can see, the chart on P/E history is an inversion of the interest rate chart.

Price/Earnings Multiple S&P 500

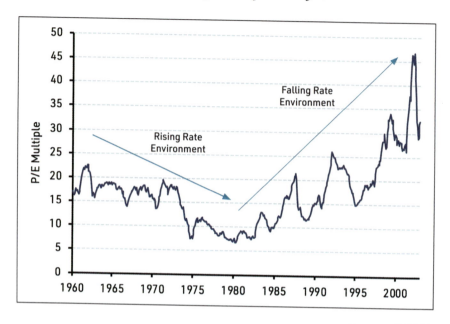

Source: SCCM.

GETTING STARTED

NEW INVESTORS

FOR READERS LOOKING to get into the market for the first time, this last chapter may be the book's most interesting. We introduce the subject of compound interest, which Albert Einstein once called "the eighth wonder of the world." It's also been called "the great miracle of stock ownership."

But compound interest does not get much attention on Wall Street, preoccupied as it is with Bitcoin, meme stocks, wild swings in the FANG stocks, and speculation about what Washington politicians might do next.

Meanwhile, neither the importance of compound interest nor any meaningful instruction in personal financial planning is offered in our schools. Students might benefit, for example, from studying what happened to the Florida doctors covered in Chapter 8. In that instructive example, young people could learn that starting with a small amount of money, adding to it every year with more small amounts, and sticking to a discipline for the long term, can produce truly dramatic results. This is what is meant by compounding.

Examples of Compounded Interest at Work

The three examples below demonstrate the power of compounding.

14-Year-Old Paper Boy or Girl

Assumption: $1,000 starting value

Annual Return: 10%

Annual Contribution: $1,040, $20/week first 10yrs, $10k/year after

In this example, our young person starts with $1,000 at age 14. Perhaps a Thanksgiving or Christmas gift from an aunt, uncle, or grandparent.

They invest this and earn an annual return of 10%.

They continue to make investment contributions of $20 per week for 10 years, until reaching their mid-20s, and then $10,000 per year after that when they enter employment.

As the table shows, if they keep this up until age 80 they will have in excess of $24 million.

Age	Value
14	$1,080
20	$8,756
30	$101,115
40	$437,577
50	$1,310,273
60	$3,573,823
70	$9,444,888
80	$24,672,918

25-Year-Old

Assumption: $50,000 starting value

Annual Return: 10%

Annual Contribution: $10,000

In this example, our 25-year-old enters the workforce. To date, he has saved up $50,000 from student jobs and family gifts.

From age 25 onwards, $10,000 per year is invested until age 80, at which time he will have approximately $31 million.

Age	Value
25	$54,000
30	$131,577
40	$516,587
50	$1,582,362
60	$4,454,863
70	$11,905,390
80	$31,230,139

40-Year-Old Couple

Assumption: $200,000 starting value

Annual Return: 10%

Annual Contribution: $30,000 ($15,000 each)

In this example, our couple had some savings by the time they reached 40 years of age, but wanted to save additionally.

Our couple invests $200,000 at 10%, and then $30,000 per year from then on, until they hit age 80. At that time the investment will have growth to over $17 million.

Age	Value
40	$216,000
50	$707,497
60	$2,361,000
70	$6,649,761
80	$17,703,772

Reasons Not To Invest

Another problem for the person who thinks they want to get started in investing is that it never seems like the ideal time. The market might look too expensive, or the economic or political environment might seem especially negative and uncertain. Getting potential investors started was always a big problem when I began my career on Wall Street at Merrill Lynch.

But a colleague and an old pro stepped in to help. He gave me the list below of all the years from 1934 to 1990 and for each year there is a major reason not to invest. Even so, the market moved steadily higher over the 56 years.

Not much has changed in the 31 years since 1990; every year there has been another reason. The market in 2021 may seem too high; and in 2020, there was the Covid pandemic and a contentious presidential election. But the stock market, driven by earnings, has moved steadily higher.

There Are Always "Reasons" Not To Invest

1934	Depression	1963	Kennedy assassinated
1935	Spanish Civil War	1964	Gulf of Tonkin
1936	Economy still struggling	1965	Civil rights marches
1937	Recession	1966	Vietnam War escalates
1938	War clouds gather	1967	Newark race riots
1939	War in Europe	1968	USS *Pueblo* seized
1940	France falls	1969	Money tightens—markets *full*
1941	Pearl Harbor	1970	Cambodia invaded—Vietnam War spreads
1942	Wartime price controls		
1943	Industry mobilizes	1971	Wage price freeze
1944	Consumer goods shortages	1972	Largest US trade deficit ever
1945	Post-war recession predicted	1973	Energy crisis
1946	Dow tops 200—market *too* high	1974	Steepest market drop in four decades
1947	Cold War begins	1975	Clouded economic prospects
1948	Berlin blockade	1976	Economic recovery slows
1949	Russia explodes A-bomb	1977	Market slumps
1950	Korean War	1978	Interest rates rise
1951	Excess Profits Tax	1979	Oil prices skyrocket
1952	US seizes steel mills	1980	Interest rates at all-time high
1953	Russia explodes H-bomb	1981	Steep recession begins
1954	Dow tops 300—market *too* high	1982	Worst recession in 40 years
1955	Eisenhower illness	1983	Market hits new highs
1956	Suez Crisis	1984	Record federal deficits
1957	Russia launches Sputnik	1985	Economic growth slows
1958	Recession	1986	Dow nears 2,000
1959	Castro seizes power in Cuba	1987	Record-setting market decline
1960	Russia downs U-2 plane	1988	Election year
1961	Berlin Wall erected	1989	October "Mini-Crash"
1962	Cuban Missile Crisis	1990	Persian Gulf crisis

"Now Is Always The Hardest Time To Invest..."

—Bernard Mannes Baruch, Presidential adviser and financial analyst

Source: SCCM.

Is Timing Important?

How about the timing of making contributions?

John Templeton did a study, covered earlier, that examined a 22-year period from 1969 to 1991, which showed that if you made an investment on the best day of the year rather than the worst, the difference over the time period was only 1%. So the key to making additional investments, as well as getting started in the first place, was not to be distracted by the passing gyrations of the market and daily newspaper headlines.

The key to building wealth is get started, make steady contributions, be disciplined as to price, and stay the course.

FINAL NOTE

The following major points can summarize the book:

1. Investing with a discipline—price-to-equity, price-to-book and dividend yield—gives investors a huge advantage over time.

2. Being a long-term investor, i.e., five years, goes a long way to reduce the market's year-to-year volatility.

3. Investors must be on constant alert to avoid the temptation to try to time the market.

APPENDIX: CALCULATION METHODOLOGY FOR CHAPTER 2 STUDY

Top/Bottom 20% by P/E

All members of the S&P 500 on December 31 of current year (year n) are ranked into quintiles by the current year Price-to-Earnings (P/E) defined as: December 31 closing price for year n divided by Basic EPS excluding Extraordinary Items and Discontinued Operations as reported for year n. In the event of a company with zero earnings or negative earnings, the company is moved to the highest P/E quintile and the quintiles are readjusted to equal quintiles. In the event of an identical P/E between two or more companies, the matching P/E companies will then be sorted alphabetically in their current positions. The year n+1 return for each quintile is a simple average of the year n+1 total return for each quintile member. The top 20% by P/E is the return for the highest P/E quintile. The bottom 20% by P/E is the return for the lowest P/E quintile.

Top/Bottom 20% by P/B

All members of the S&P 500 on December 31 of current year (year n) are ranked into quintiles by the current year Price-to-Book ratio (P/B) defined as December 31 closing price for year n divided by Book Value per share as reported for year n. In the event of a company with zero book value or negative book value, the company is moved to the highest P/B quintile and the quintiles are readjusted to equal quintiles. In the event of an identical P/B between two or more companies, the matching P/B companies will then be sorted alphabetically in their current positions. The year n+1 return for each quintile is a simple average of the year n+1 total return for each quintile member. The top 20% by P/B is the return for the highest P/B quintile. The bottom 20% by P/B is the return for the lowest P/B quintile.

Top 20% by Dividend Yield

All members of the S&P 500 on December 31 of current year (year n) are ranked into quintiles by the current fiscal year Dividend Yield (DY) defined as Cash Dividends per Share paid for year n divided by December 31 closing price for year n. A 0.0% DY is assigned to companies that did not pay any dividends in year n. In the event of an identical DY between two or more companies, the matching DY companies will then be sorted alphabetically in their current positions. The year n+1 return for each quintile is a simple average of the year n+1 total return for each quintile member. The top 20% by DY is the return for the highest yielding quintile.

ACKNOWLEDGMENTS

First, I want to mention my appreciation for my wife Gail and her back up of three yellow labs. Throughout this process over the last three years she has had to deal with the ups and downs of all kinds of unexpected events like office closures, city closures, etc. It took a lot of patience.

As for the book, I first want to compliment Ashley Hicks who did a phenomenal job with typewriting this book from beginning to end. As a writer, I do not use a computer or the famous "yellow pad," so the only medium I use is to recite the material, and of course, the secret is to be able to have someone who can type as fast as you can speak, and Ashley was able to do that in spades. Also, Stephen O'Neil of Schafer Cullen was very helpful in reviewing the final drafts of the book, and he and Ashley did a great job of working with the editor on making the various changes despite the fact that the editor was in a different time zone and on the other side of the ocean.

Special thanks to Grant Ujifusa, formally of Random House, who has done line editing with me over the last 20 years with my market letters. He was working with me when we started with the book and has been very helpful and supportive in the whole process.

Obviously, getting the right publishing firm is important. We interviewed quite a few firms and finally selected the highly regarded Harriman House, which specializes only in financial books. The reason why we chose them is because Craig Pearce was going to be our editor. We were happy with our choice as Craig did a phenomenal job with us and made the whole process a pleasant experience.

Special praise goes to Ed Murphy, CFA of Schafer Cullen, who is responsible for the financial numbers in the book and to Anuca Laudat, CFA and Mike Gallant, CFA for chasing down background information for the book. Also thanks to Jason Steinberg who is responsible for a lot of the charts.

INDEX